D1505628

ROADSIGNS

ROADSIGNS

NAVIGATING YOUR
PATH TO SPIRITUAL HAPPINESS

PHILIP GOLDBERG, PH.D.

RODALE

© 2003 by Philip Goldberg
Cover Photograph © by Kaz Mori/Getty Images

Printed in the United States of America
Rodale Inc. makes every effort to use acid-free ∞, recycled paper ♻ .

Book design by Joanna Williams

Library of Congress Cataloging-in-Publication Data

Goldberg, Philip, date.
    Roadsigns : navigating your path to spiritual happiness / Philip Goldberg.
        p.   cm.
    ISBN 1–57954–588–2   hardcover
    1. Spiritual life.   I. Title.
    BL624 .G6342 2003
    291.4'4—dc21   2002153810

Distributed to the book trade by St. Martin's Press

2   4   6   8   10 9 7 5 3 1   hardcover

Visit us on the Web at www.rodalestore.com, or call us toll-free at (800) 848-4735.

WE **INSPIRE** AND **ENABLE** PEOPLE TO IMPROVE
THEIR LIVES AND THE WORLD AROUND THEM

To Lori, my copilot,
with whom I travel the path in love.

ACKNOWLEDGMENTS

As with life on the spiritual path, an author's work is done primarily in seclusion, but it is aided immeasurably by the help of others. I wish to thank first and foremost all the teachers who have so profoundly graced my life, both in person and through their works. My thanks extend to the countless fellow travelers with whom I've discussed spiritual issues over the course of many years. I am indebted to a great many who did not know, as they chatted with me, that they were helping me research a book, because I did not know it myself at the time. I am grateful for their insights and heartfelt sharing. I thank especially those who explicitly offered ideas, moral support, and practical wisdom as this book passed from commitment to realization. In alphabetical order: Harold Bloomfield, Dana Brekke, Christine Chagnon, James Finley, Judy Firestone, Jack and Roberta Forem, Bob Forman, Elliot Friedland, Rachel Harris, Dick Helfant, Nikki Johnson, Diana and Doug Kruschke, Kay Lindahl, Franz Metcalf, Katherine O'Connell, Kikanza Nuri Robins, Neil Schuitevoerder, Dean Sluyter, Barbara Stevens, Jim Strohecker, Jeremy Tarcher, Sirah Vettese, Aaron Zerah, and Connie Zweig.

Special thanks to my agent and friend, Lynn Franklin, for her staunch support of my work in general and for this project in particular; and to Troy Juliar and Stephanie Tade of Rodale Books for their faith in this book and their astute editorial judgment.

Singular and profound gratitude to Lori Deutsch, my beloved companion, for the perceptive editorial insights that helped sharpen the book, and for the loving heart that sustained me through the course of the work. Finally, to my family—in particular my brother, Bob, and my departed parents, Ann and Archie—for a lifetime of love that continues to feed my spirit.

CONTENTS

To arrive at that which we know not,
we must travel by a way which we know not.
—John of the Cross

God turns you from one feeling to another,
and teaches by means of opposites,
so that you have two wings to fly, not one.
—Rumi

INTRODUCTION

My spiritual quest has, in its most significant features, mirrored the journeys of thousands of seekers in the West. As a young man, I disdained religion as I then understood it, only to become just as disillusioned by secular versions of wisdom and fulfillment. By the late 1960s, my dogged search for higher truth led to the mystical teachings of the East and, through them, to the esoteric branches of *all* traditions. After exploring widely, I was drawn to Maharishi Mahesh Yogi's Transcendental Meditation (TM); for several years I taught meditation, led retreats, lectured, and otherwise served the TM organization with zealous dedication. My motives were multifaceted, but a major one was the promise of "two hundred percent of life"—one hundred percent spiritual, one hundred percent worldly—which was made to seem like an easily attainable goal. It turned out not to be.

Eventually, I withdrew from that association and continued my search for the elusive two hundred percent as a spiritual freelancer. Ever since, I have wrestled incessantly with this fundamental question: How can one pursue the Divine with diligence while living fully in the material world? Not just *the* material world, but *our* material world, which seems so incompatible with genuine spirituality.

Along the way I learned that, regardless of the

specifics of their journeys, all seekers struggle with the same basic issues. We stumble into similar mysteries for which we have no ready answer, and we are forced to make decisions for which we are unprepared. As inevitable as bad weather, these dilemmas sometimes crop up at the beginning of the road, sometimes once the expedition is well underway and the wonder and excitement begin to fade, and sometimes years or decades later, when we have been lulled into complacency by a period of contentment.

Some of the quandaries with which we grapple have been shared by seekers since the first moment a human being asked, "What am I doing here? What's it all about?" Others are peculiar to our time and place. This is partly because many of the practices and precepts that inform our paths come from traditions that have, for centuries, been geared to monastic life, or else were formulated in simple cultures vastly different from our own. In addition to being susceptible to distortions, these teachings are, in many respects, out of sync with a complex, pluralistic society that is marked by materialism, sensory bombardment, and almost infinite freedom of choice. I recently heard about a holy man on his first day in America. When asked what he would like to eat, the monk looked at his hosts in utter befuddlement: The concept of choosing one's meals from a cornucopia of possibilities was inconceivable to him. One shudders to think what might happen to his serenity if he had to choose a long-distance service.

Another source of today's dilemmas is also one of our greatest assets: the staggering array of spiritual teachings that are available to everyone. While this is an unprecedented opportunity for richness, depth, and the creation of individually tailored paths, it is also mind-boggling. Authorities contradict each other, and sometimes themselves. Concepts that once illumined our way now lead to cul-de-sacs of paradox and ambiguity. Yesterday's truth becomes today's confusion and tomorrow's hogwash—and vice versa. Where do you look for guidance? Whom do you trust? How do you make decisions?

Adapting perennial wisdom to modern sensibility is, and probably always will be, a work in progress. Meanwhile, those of us who heed the eternal call of the spirit can only shuffle toward enlightenment as best we can. We muddle through, decoding one mystery after another, trying to render unto God and Caesar alike without offending either. To be sure, there are times when the road is friction-free and bump-proof. The ride is joyful, even blissful. Inner and outer are of a piece, and decisions are not so much made as glided into. Then, almost inevitably, comes a bone-rattling pothole, a traffic jam, a detour, a collision. You feel bogged down by doubt and confusion. You don't know which way to turn, or whether to exit completely. That's when you understand why the spiritual path has been called a razor's edge, and why the sublime promises of sacred texts are tempered with cautionary statements like this one from the Bhagavad Gita: "Hazardous and slow is the path to the Unrevealed, difficult for physical man to tread."

This book was written to help seekers steer through the hazards on the sacred highway. It is intended to fit into the backpack or glove compartment, so to speak, of everyone who takes spirituality seriously, whether he or she has been at it for thirty days or thirty years. My goal is to ease your way along the path, whether it is mainstream or unconventional, whether independent or within an established institution. The book will help you become more savvy and self-aware, better prepared to make sound decisions.

The book is arranged in four sections, each organized around one of the major paradoxes that mark the spiritual path. Each chapter addresses an important issue that seekers typically encounter. The goal is to help you come to conclusions that best serve your needs at every moment. The chapter titles are phrased as roadsigns, so they can serve as handy aphorisms to remind you of essential points once their meaning has been absorbed.

Each chapter is meant to be digestible in a single sitting. In addition to the main discussions, which cover all sides of the issue at hand, the chapters contain memorable, incisive quotes from a variety of sources, plus a section headed Travel Tips, with exercises, action steps, questions to ask oneself, and a statement or passage to contemplate. Some chapters also contain stories to illuminate major ideas and sidebars that highlight alternative viewpoints or important caveats. The book contains solid, practical advice gleaned from more than thirty years of personal experience and research, but its primary goal is to lead you toward the best kind of guidance you can find: that which springs from your own self-awareness and personal insight.

I believe the book will help you:

- Discover your personal truths as you move toward the Ultimate Truth
- Relieve your doubt and confusion
- Arrive at fresh new insights

- Gain inspiration and new skills
- Know more about yourself and your spiritual needs
- Carve out a path that is right for you
- Become better equipped to continue your quest with grace and dignity.

The promises of the spiritual life—peace, joy, love, wisdom, intimacy with the Divine—are real. They are attainable. The way to them is simpler and more direct than some would have you believe—and also more arduous and more baffling than is often depicted. The path is both as serious as a sermon and as wacky as a sitcom. It is my hope that this book will lighten your load and help you enjoy your journey at every step—and, in the words of the yogic sage Patanjali, "Avoid the danger that has not yet come." Happy trails.

ROADSIGNS

YOU'RE
ON YOUR OWN

I lift up my eyes to the hills.
From whence does my help come?
—Psalm 121:1

The Great Way has no gate.
There are a thousand different paths.
Once you pass through the barrier,
you walk the universe alone.
—Wu-men

On the spiritual path, we are alone and we are together. We need mapmakers, guides, and companions, for the road is uncertain and the signs ambiguous. Yet we each have to be our own mapmaker, our own guide, and, ultimately, our best and only companion. No matter how faithful we are to a teaching or a higher power, no matter how excellent our guides, each of us is the final choice-maker. This is especially true if we walk an independent path, but also if we follow a tradition. To choose well, we have to use our heads—and follow our hearts. We have to think hard—and stop thinking so hard. We have to respect our intellects—and trust our intuition.

YOU CAN'T
DO IT ALONE

1

MAPS MAY NOT APPLY; CHART YOUR OWN COURSE

God enters by a private door into every individual.
—*Ralph Waldo Emerson*

At a formative period in my spiritual journey, the Bhagavad Gita was the focal point of study in my circle of seekers. Like other scriptures, the ancient text was a Rorschach of sorts: Each individual seemed to be drawn to a particular verse or verses. During conversations, we would often quote our favorite lines to make a point. We remembered them because they resonated with our psyches, and we turned to them repeatedly for inspiration or deeper reflection. For some, the favored passage emphasized service; for others, it was one that evoked reverence for God or stressed the importance of diligent practice. Mine was: "Because one can perform it, one's own dharma, though lesser in merit, is better than the dharma of another. Better is death in one's own dharma: the dharma of another brings danger."

Dharma, a central concept in both Hindu and Buddhist teachings, is a complex term with a number of meanings. In this context, it refers to actions that are most conducive to one's spiritual development. At the time, the verse strengthened my resolve to do what I felt was right for me at every step rather than to submit without scrutiny to a dogma or a dictum. I would return to it again and again, whenever I found myself at a crossroad.

It has not always been easy to distinguish my true dharma from some ego-serving delusion or a cowardly cop-out. But it always seemed safer and wiser to err on the side of authenticity. Each time I failed to live up to the spirit of that verse, I later regretted it.

> *Know well what leads you forward and what holds you back, and choose the path that leads to wisdom.*
> —Buddha

It might seem arrogant or self-important to say, "I'm in charge of my spiritual voyage," when you know perfectly well that you need all the help you can get. We need to humbly admit the limits of our knowledge. We need to have faith in sources wiser than ourselves and to remain open to the time-tested authority of tradition. We need to listen for the higher wisdom of divine intelligence. But ultimately the buck stops with each of us.

You are the pilot and navigator on your spiritual path. Only you can decide whether to seek advice, where to look for it, and whether or not to follow it. Only you can interpret the sacred signposts and sort through their apparent contradictions. Only you can determine how the wisdom of the ages fits your circumstances. You are the final decision maker, and your ultimate compass is your own sense of truth. On the spiritual path there are no one-size-fits-all itineraries.

Certainly, there are seekers for whom strict obedience to a teacher or a spiritual institution is the right and proper way. But even they must determine for themselves the exact terms of their discipleship. They and only they can decide how the teachings to which they pledge their faith apply to their lives and where their lines of surrender shall be drawn. Wrote the Christian contemplative Thomas Merton, "Obedience is not the abdication of freedom but its *prudent use* under certain well-defined conditions." Your choice may be to "let go and let God," or to surrender wholeheartedly to a master, but still, that choice is yours and only yours, and you and only you will have to keep on making that choice—or not make it— every step of the way.

To be sure, there are pitfalls to declaring yourself captain of your spiritual ship. It is easy to use "I have to be true to myself" as a way to rationalize sloth, ego gratification, or the hell-bent pursuit of worldly desires—in which case you might very well slow down your spiritual growth in the name of speeding it up. Many people, for instance, misapply Joseph Campbell's famous advice to "Follow your bliss," opting at every turn for ease and pleasure while neglecting the hard work that might bring them to *real* bliss. We often belt out "My Way" when "Thy will be done" might be the more productive tune. But it is also true that following expert advice can hold you back if, in the attempt, you have to force yourself to be something you're not. On the one hand, you might turn your back on the radical challenge of spiritual transformation; on the other, you might force yourself onto a Procrustean bed of prescribed behavior and either squeeze your spirit to death or stretch it till it snaps.

Here is the balancing point: Can you take the hand of the pathfinders without losing sight of who you really are? Can you accept that there is a great deal you don't know and, at the same time, accept the equally daunting truth that every decision comes back to your desk whether you feel qualified or not? Can you hold on to your power without becoming arrogant, and without deluding yourself or cutting yourself off from sources of greater wisdom?

> *A chick's legs, though short, cannot be lengthened without discomfort to the duck: a crane's legs, through long, cannot be shortened without discomfort to the crane.*
> —Chuang-Tzu

In the mythology of India, stories are told of the young Lord Krishna's irresistible appeal to the female cowherds known as *gopis*. In these allegorical tales, the passion for the Divine, as represented by Krishna, is shaped by each gopi's perception of the beloved. Wishing to please them all, Krishna takes on forms and qualities that would satisfy each. The stories imply that the innate yearning for holy union takes on a great many shapes. All traditions have developed a number of pathways to accommodate variations in personality and preference. One way of categorizing these differences is by these four types:

1. *The path of the mind.* What is called *jnana yoga* in India is a road best traveled by those inclined to study scripture and contemplate ideas. In its purest form, this path trains the student to distinguish the real from the unreal, the eternal from the perishable, the truly sacred from the illusory. The goal is not just to understand, but to transport the mind beyond itself.

2. *The path of the heart.* Worship, devotion, and love are the hallmarks of this road (*bhakti yoga*). It is favored by those who are driven more by feeling than by thought. The object of worship might be a god-like incarnation such as Jesus or Krishna, a figure from religious history, a deity, or a living person such as a guru—any of who might be adored as a representative of the ultimate Reality. For some seekers, a spouse, a child, or the unspoiled natural world is the focal point of devotion. In any case, it is self-less love that lights the way to the Holy.

3. *The path of action.* Favored by individuals who are drawn to the pursuit of worthy goals, this approach (*karma yoga*) demands ego-free detachment from the fruits of one's efforts. Those attracted to this way are called upon to work for a higher good, whether in service to a teacher or an institution or to charitable activities in the community, with no thought of personal gain. They are to serve selflessly, as if every action were an offering to the Divine.

4. *The psycho-physiological path.* What might be considered a variation of *raja yoga,* this pragmatic road to spiritual development emphasizes the disciplined application of mental and physical practices. Meditation, prayer, chanting, breathing exercises, and the like are used to open the mind to the Sacred and to cultivate the capacity to sustain higher states of awareness.

Most aspirants incorporate elements of all four pathways, while emphasizing one over the others—and that emphasis might shift as one's developmental needs change. Because the mix of personal history, heredity, and social influences that make each of us unique is so complex, there are, in a very real sense, an infinite number of

PENCIL IT IN

*Knowledge is different in
different states of consciousness.*
—Rig-Veda

As we grow spiritually, virtually everything that factors into our decision making is subject to change. Our intellects change with every new insight and every fresh slice of wisdom. Our hearts change as they open to greater love and compassion. Our bodies change as we tap into inner peace and refine our perceptual apparatus. Our likes and dislikes, our needs and desires, our dominant feelings, our relationships with others—all change as we shed the skin of one stage of development and don another. Old assumptions are called into question. Truths we thought were eternal scream

paths to the Divine, one for each traveler. It is as if we were all enrolled in the same school but have each been assigned a personalized curriculum.

> *We can only learn to know ourselves and do what we can—namely, surrender our will and fulfill God's will in us.*
> —St. Teresa of Avila

At every step on the spiritual path you are pulled this way and that. You are given sage advice, but applying it might not feel right. You receive commandments, but they don't necessarily make sense. You read or hear something revelatory but later think, "How does it work in *my* life?" You try to be a "good" Christian, Jew, Muslim, or Buddhist, or to follow the dictates of a teacher or scripture, but the guidelines turn out to be ambiguous. In our com-out for review. And with every change, we have to adapt. Not only must every choice be made according to the truth of who we are at the moment, but that truth itself must be constantly updated and reevaluated.

It is extremely important, therefore, not to get locked into a fixed self-image. You are not the same person you were when you started your spiritual voyage. You are not even the same person you were when you opened this book. So how can you assume that what was right for you yesterday is right for you today, or that what's right for you today will be right for you tomorrow? Because you can function only from the state of awareness you're in at any given time, you have to be ready to shift the angle of the steering wheel—sometimes radically, sometimes imperceptibly, sometimes quickly, sometimes gradually. All phenomena are eternally changing, including the individual you call "me."

plex world, with its overlapping roles, competing values, and virtually infinite choices, being true to yourself can be a mind-boggling, sometimes paralyzing, challenge.

The burden can feel so heavy you want to shout to the heavens, "Lift this from my shoulders. Just show me what to do." At the same time, realizing that the buck stops with you can be liberating. Perhaps that is one of the symbolic lessons in Jesus' insistence on carrying his own cross. Accepting that responsibility can keep you from settling for spiritual bromides or relinquishing your power. It forces you to honor the integrity of your experience, the wisdom of your intuition, and the sanctity of your own logic, so you can make decisions that are honest for you at every turn. You won't always make the right choice. But if you pay attention, even your mistakes—perhaps *especially* your mistakes—will lift you to the next step.

TRAVEL TIPS

1. Write out your answers to the following questions:

- How would you describe the purpose of your path?
- On a spiritual level, what do you yearn for most?
- How would you describe your biggest spiritual challenge?

2. On a scale of one to five, how important is it to maintain your spiritual independence? On a scale of one to five, how willing are you to adopt the advice of spiritual authorities?

If you scored higher on the first question, is it because you are happily autonomous or because you are resistant to authority? If you scored higher on the second, is it because you have faith in traditions and leaders, or because you don't trust yourself?

3. What do you do when you are torn between what's right for you on the one hand and tradition, teacher, or text on the other? If you find yourself leaning toward acquiescence, ask yourself:

- Am I humbly yielding to a higher wisdom because it is likely to lead to blessings?
- Or, am I giving myself less respect than I deserve?
- Am I afraid I'll be ostracized if I don't go along?

If, on the other hand, you are tempted to follow your own counsel and defy authoritative advice, ask yourself:

- Am I listening to the most authentic part of myself?
- Am I taking the easy way out?
- Am I afraid I won't measure up to spiritual demands?

4. Contemplate this passage from the philosopher and novelist Aldous Huxley: "To know the ultimate Not-Self, which transcends the other not-selves and the ego, but which is yet closer than breathing, nearer than hands and feet—this is the consummation of human life, the end and ultimate purpose of human existence."

2

FORKS IN THE ROAD: YIELD RIGHT OF WAY

Live at the empty heart of paradox.
I'll dance with you there, cheek to cheek.
—*Rumi*

Imagine taking a cross-country trip on the back roads of America with a map of the entire country as your only guide. The Big Picture would be clear. The overall design of the journey would be well-charted. But you would not know where to turn at specific junctures. Suppose you came to an intersection and found two traffic cops, each pointing in a different direction. Imagine asking for assistance and hearing, "Turn right at the next light, or maybe left. It depends." Suppose well-meaning bystanders jumped in with contradictory opinions: "Go straight for two miles." "No, six." "You're both crazy, it's *that* way!" "Don't listen to them. My way is the *only* way." Imagine that when you asked certain questions, you were told, "Sorry, that is unknowable."

At times, the spiritual path is a lot like that. Uncertainty is a constant companion, and the landscape is marked by contradiction, ambiguity, and paradox.

This is inevitable. The very nature of existence—

whether defined by science or religion—is contradictory, ambiguous, and paradoxical. It is also, to a large extent, unknowable. The universe is made up of certain properties and, at the same time, the *opposites* of those properties; subatomic particles behave like both waves and solid objects; that electrons orbit the nucleus of atoms because the forces of attraction and repulsion are perfectly balanced—just as Earth stays in orbit for the same reason. The Ultimate Reality that many call God is said to be formless and also contained within form; unchanging and also infinitely varied; transcendent and also immanent; infinitely merciful and also fiercely judgmental; omnipresent and also separate from us.

As for human beings, we were formed from dust and are savage as beasts—and created in the Almighty's image, animated by the breath of the Divine, as noble as gods. Our time on earth is as fleeting as a gust of wind and yet everything we do is of great significance. We are apart from nature and a part of nature. We are, each of us, separate and unique, and we are also one and inseparable. We are embodied in material form, and we are also pure spirit—localized in time and space, and also infinite and eternal.

On the spiritual path, this waltz of opposites is often experienced as profound ambivalence. We are told that we are already enlightened, but that we have miles to go and lifetimes to live before we come to that supreme realization. We are told that the universe is exactly as it should be, but that it is our duty to make it better; that each of us is perfect, but we're also imperfect beings programmed to grow; that we are forgiven, but we have to earn forgiveness; that we're on a path, but there's nowhere to go. We are told that God is love and the Self is bliss, yet we suffer, and innocents are slaughtered and communities are destroyed by "acts of God." It is said that we have free will, and also that everything is written. Scriptures tell us to renounce the mundane world as base or illusory, and also to treat it with utmost gravity and embrace it as holy. And on and on, in a dizzying whirl of contradiction.

> *Our minds are perpetually shifting in and out of confusion and clarity. If only we were confused all the time, that would at least make for some kind of clarity.*
> —*Sogyal Rinpoche*

Of course, you can eliminate uncertainty and sidestep ambiguity any time you want to. You can take refuge in dogma or doctrine, cult or clergy, or any authority that offers unequivocal answers. That can be a tempting option; the mind craves certainty like a weary traveler longs for a cozy inn and good hot meal. No wonder so many find respite in the fervent assurances of fundamentalism. There are times in almost every seeker's life when clinging to orthodox rules is a luxury too gracious to resist, if only as temporary relief. But, as Joseph Campbell pointed out, one of the problems with conventional religion is that it can work against its deeper purpose by serving as an "inoculation against the Divine:" its comforting certainties protect you from having to face the Mystery in all its awesome majesty.

In the long run, any honest seeker who thinks for him- or herself comes back to the cold, unambiguous truth that, while certain spiritual premises are universal and inviolable, virtually every guiding principle one comes across can be modified by "Yes, but . . ." "Except when . . ." "On the other hand . . ." and similar quali-fiers.

As we muddle through, the points of certainty and uncertainty shift, as do the points of clarity and contra-diction. Yesterday's life-changing, not-to-be-doubted, soul-shifting revelation becomes today's enigma and to-morrow's rubbish. And vice versa, as today's rubbish turns miraculously into tomorrow's revelation. Even the most sacred of sources can disappoint the seeker of unadulterated truth. "You can't treat the Bible like a ref-erence manual to simply look up information about God," says Karen Armstrong, author of *A History of God,* "because you're likely to find your data contra-dicted on the next page."

Perhaps the balance point is best found in the cer-tainty of uncertainty and in the brave acceptance of am-bivalence as a companion on the path. This may seem to be a curse, but it can be a blessing. In most worthwhile journeys it is the surprises we remember most vividly and recall with the greatest excitement—and not just the shockers that delighted us at the time, but also those that annoyed us and frightened us, because they led to unex-pected treasures, to valuable lessons, and sometimes, to grace.

Perhaps the healthiest attitude is to surrender to the Mystery—to yield to it, embrace it, and marvel at it, like a volunteer from the audience at a magic show. For that is, in a sense, what we are: witnesses to cosmic hocus-pocus whose secrets we are not privy to. The sooner we stop trying to figure out how the magician put the rabbit back in the hat, the sooner we can achieve what the poet

John Keats called negative capability: "being in uncertainties, mysteries, doubts, without any irritable reaching after facts and reason." This does not amount to resignation or existential apathy. Rather, it is both a pragmatic strategy and a profound spiritual practice. Not knowing—what Zen calls "beginner's mind"—can be liberating because it calls upon us to stop grasping for answers that can't be found. It helps us to pry loose from entrenched ideas, opinions, and assumptions. It brings not only a measure of peace, but also a certain glee—that magic show glee—and it opens a door to new and startling possibilities.

The same is true when we yield to ambiguity, like a diver who gracefully surrenders to gravity. In science a paradox is often regarded as nature's way of trying to tell us something about herself—or, more accurately, about the way we've been thinking about her. Calling a truce in the seesaw battle between contradictory ideas creates an opening for a "sacred third" to arise from the creative tension. But it happens only when we give up our urgent attachment to the outcome and get out of the way.

> Our mission is to recognize contraries for what they are: first of all as contraries, but then as opposite poles of a unity.
> —Hermann Hesse

Like our wandering ancestors, spiritual seekers often find themselves adrift in a mental wilderness, looking for the promised land of truth and equilibrium. In this landscape, which holds the possibility of danger as well as the promise of deliverance, letting go of the need for closure is, in a very real sense, a spiritual practice. Like the leap

CAUTION: ORACLE MAY BE OUT OF SERVICE

The fact that logic cannot satisfy us awakens an almost insatiable hunger for the irrational.
—A. N. Wilson

Faced with paralyzing ambivalence, many seekers turn to esoteric assistance: astrologers, psychics, channelers, readers of tarot cards, and other soothsayers who are presumably plugged in to a cosmic database the rest of us can't access. Used sensibly, they can be seen as experts with specialized skills and knowledge, like accountants, technicians, or plumbers; we can benefit from their services if we examine what they have to say and weigh it against other points of view. The trouble comes when we bestow upon them an excess of authority.

I have seen otherwise sensible people turn over their power to such advisers, only to regret it later on. One hard-headed businesswoman, for example, prides herself on being decisive. When it comes to men, however, she no longer trusts her judgment. So, she does what her psychic tells her to do. Unfortunately, her heart continues to be broken on a

of faith made by the first Hebrew to set foot in the parted Red Sea, it acknowledges the immensity of our ignorance and the need to trust in a higher intelligence. Surrendering to the ineffable mysteries of life can be seen as an exercise in nonattachment, since the need for certainty is just another form of craving. As we pass, like a driver changing lanes, from knowing to not-knowing, from conviction to contradiction, it pays to remember a fundamental spiri-

regular basis, while her Midas touch in business remains flawless. Then there's the couple that had one happy year together, and spent the next four like prisoners on a chain gang who can't kill each other but can't separate either. Why did they stay together? Because an astrologer said that their horoscopes were perfectly compatible. Therefore, the marriage was meant to be, and their difficulties were part of their lesson plan. Finally, unable to stand it any longer, they got a second opinion and are now happily divorced.

If you turn to occult helpers, keep in mind:

1. They're not infallible. As a friend of mine said about the entities channeled by a medium, "Just because they're dead doesn't make them smart."
2. They're subject to interpretation. Like dreams, their messages can be so riddle-like that the meaning is not obvious.
3. They might be feeding your ego. Perhaps you find their messages irresistible because they elevate your self-image or paint a rosy picture of the future.
4. You might be sending a debilitating message to your subconscious mind: "I need outside help because I can't count on myself."

tual teaching: Everything on this earthly plane is impermanent, even some of our most cherished concepts and our most confident assertions.

If we can get to that happy and courageous state of surrender authentically—without confusing the certainty of uncertainty with a lack of discernment or the fear of taking a stand—we open ourselves to something bordering on the miraculous. Where better to find Union than in the coexistence of opposites? What better place to find the Unknowable than where things are not entirely known? What better time to confront the Unfathomable than when you can't fathom what's going on? Like a mind-boggled Zen novice who gives up grappling with a koan (the logic-transcending riddles used by masters as a teaching tool), we just might come to rest in silence. And it is there, in silence, where the deepest wisdom is to be found. Not just answers to real-life conundrums, but the only true response we can have when we stand naked before the wonder of the created universe: awe.

TRAVEL TIPS

1. *Step off the pendulum.* When your mind swings back and forth from "On the one hand" to "On the other hand," try to observe the predicament with the detachment of a spectator. Marvel at its insolvability. Uncertainty creates a gap in the mind. Instead of seeing it as a frightening abyss, regard it as a womb in which the miracle of revelation can come to term.

2. *Post a reminder.* When the mind is struggling to find solid ground, remembering that uncertainty and ambivalence are inevitable can help you relinquish the urgency. Stick reminders where you're likely to see them—on the refrigerator door, the bathroom mirror, your desk, etc. Here are some useful quotes to choose from:

- "Live the questions now. Perhaps then . . . you will gradually, without even noticing it, live your way into the answer."—Rainer Maria Rilke

- "Getting the knack of relaxing in the midst of chaos, learning not to panic—this is the spiritual path."—Pema Chodron

- "Life is not a problem to be solved but a mystery to be lived."—Joe Ripley Caldwell

Or, try these unintentional koans from that famous Yogi, Berra:

- "When you come to a fork in the road, take it."

- "If you don't know where you're going, you might not get there."

3. *Check in with your feelings.* Sometimes mental confusion springs from turbulent emotions. When the heart is conflicted, the mind, with its need for equilibrium, searches for a reasonable explanation. Try to identify the underlying emotions and resolve them.

4. *Do an ego check*. In America, where pollsters ask ordinary people about matters that stump experts and friends expect you to review a movie before you reach the lobby, the need to have an opinion is like an infectious disease. It's as if saying "I don't know" were a sign of weakness instead of the beginning of wisdom. Here's another lesson from Swami Berra. When asked, "Don't you know anything?" Yogi is said to have replied, "I don't even suspect anything."

5. Contemplate this famous Zen saying: "Things are not what they appear to be. Nor are they otherwise."

3

KEEP INTUITION IN VIEW AT ALL TIMES

Truth is within ourselves, it takes no rise
From outward things, whate'er you may believe ...
—Robert Browning

The spectacular advance of knowledge and technological progress ushered in by the scientific method has produced an ideological bias: we venerate reason and denigrate its sister, intuition. This is reflected in our very language, where "rational" is synonymous with sanity and "reasonable" and "logical" are the benchmarks for truth. But the spiritual path exposes the limits of rational intelligence like a steep hill exposes the limits of roller skates.

Where information is incomplete and ambiguous, where analysis is forced to proceed from premises that can't be verified, the tools of reason are usually insufficient. And those conditions are built into the spiritual path. In the deepest realms of inquiry, mysteries defy the rules of logic and evade the dogged pursuit of rational minds. That is one reason why attempts to either prove or disprove the existence of God have convinced exactly no one. The problem is not that scientific rationality is so highly valued; it plainly deserves to be. Rather, the trouble is 1) its limitations tend to be overlooked; 2) its methods have been (illogically, irrationally, unreasonably) extended to areas like religion where they don't necessarily apply; and 3) *nonrational* ways of knowing have been so repressed that we have to remind ourselves of their value over and over again.

If you try to navigate the spiritual path by reason alone you are bound to think yourself into dead ends, detours, and endless circles of futility. Sometimes, it is best to exit at the scenic overlook of intuition.

There is nothing supernatural about intuition, and nothing about it is incompatible with reason. They are not rival kingdoms but complementary functions of one sovereign and indivisible mind. In my book, *The Intuitive Edge*, I identified six types of intuition:

1. *Discovery*. The sudden insight that reveals the answer to a baffling conundrum. These "Eureka!" moments usually arise after the unconscious mind has been primed by the desire to know something and has been fed information through observation and analysis. Often, the breakthrough arrives when least expected, when the mind is otherwise engaged.

2. *Creativity*. Instead of a singular truth or an answer to a question with only one solution, creative intuition generates alternatives where more than one is possible. The revelation produced is not correct in the factual sense, but something fresh and unusual, yet appropriate to the situation. This is the intuition of brainstorming and artistic fertility.

3. *Evaluation*. A binary function that whispers (or screams) "Yes" or "No," "Do it" or "Don't do it," etc.,

when you are faced with a choice. The moment of truth might come after a long period of rumination, when you can no longer put off the decision and your gut finally tips the scales. It might also come when you have to act quickly and there is no time for fact gathering or analysis.

4. *Operation*. This most subtle form of intuition is like a gyroscope or a radar system. It provides inner guidance, sometimes so gently that you have to pay attention to realize you're being prodded. It might tug you this way or nudge you that way, without telling you why. It might come in the form of what some might call a "sign" or as a persistent urge, a repeated feeling, or a vague intimation. Smooth operational intuition exemplifies the Taoist concept of *wu wei*, that effortlessness that Alan Watts called "not standing in your own light when working."

5. *Prediction*. This gives you glimpses into the future that mathematical projections and rational forecasting cannot provide. It's the sense of knowing that something is going to happen without having a clue as to why. It might come in a vision as clear as a snapshot or as a sense of portent whose features are as blurry as a figure in a fog.

6. *Illumination*. This most sublime form of intuition transcends the other categories. In fact, it transcends all concepts and ideas. Strictly speaking, it even transcends intuition. It refers to the apprehension of the Holy that mystics through the ages have exalted as Supreme Knowledge. Whether described as divine Presence or the light of God or Self-realization, whether labeled *samadhi, rigpa, nirvana, satori,* or any other term, this awakening to the ultimate reality is beyond the power of language to describe. In its purest form, the knowledge it unveils is not knowledge *of* anything in the usual sense. The polarity of

BEWARE OF IMPOSTERS

Consider Abraham. He hears what he assumes is the voice of God telling him to pack up everything and take off for parts unknown. Later, that same voice tells him to sacrifice his son, and he comes within a knife's blade of doing so. For the most part, things worked out all right for Abraham and his descendants. But the chances are that if you woke up your spouse and said, "Get dressed, God told me to sell the house and head out to the desert," you'd get the alarm clock thrown at you. And if you even came close to harming your child, you'd be arrested, although "God told me to" would probably tip the scales in favor of an insanity plea.

Sure, it's good to trust your inner voice, but don't be lulled into thinking it's flawless. It's not always easy to know whether the message in your head springs from divine revelation or your own psychic demons. When you find yourself especially eager to act on what *seems* to be an intuitive gift, ask yourself:

knower and known dissolves. What remains is consciousness aware of itself—in the words of the Upanishads, "soundless, formless, intangible, undying, tasteless, odorless, without beginning, without end, eternal, immutable, beyond nature."

>   *Learn to be silent. Let your quiet mind listen and absorb.*
>   —*Pythagorus*

Obviously, what I am calling illumination differs from the other types of intuition. With the others, the subconscious mind dispenses an answer or instruction in the

- Is anger, envy, fear, or some other difficult feeling distorting my thoughts?
- Do I just *want* this to be true? Could it really be wishful thinking?
- Am I being intuitive or merely impulsive?
- Do I like this idea because it feeds my ego?
- Does it represent the easy way out?
- Am I being intellectually lazy or impatient?
- Am I so uncomfortable with uncertainty that I'm latching onto the first excuse to break free?

How can you distinguish the real thing from the imposters? There is no easy formula, since everyone's intuition speaks a different language. Learn the nuances of your own intuitive voice; over time you will be able to identify the cues—verbal, visual, visceral, and others—that separate the wheat from the chaff.

form of thoughts, visions, feelings in the gut or chest, and other codes. By contrast, illumination is nonspecific and nonlocalized. It is also its own reward, the core element of a spiritual awakening that has been described as the end of ignorance, the end of alienation, and the end of suffering. But it also has practical relevance in our context because the illuminative experience transforms everyday awareness and upgrades the other five intuitive functions. This is because the spiritual practices used for bringing it about—meditation, prayer, contemplation, etc.—make the mind quieter, clearer, and less agitated, the very conditions under which intuition flourishes. Stillness creates an ideal backdrop against which the notes of divine wisdom can be discerned. Some call it the voice of God.

This gives spiritual practitioners a distinct advantage when it comes to cultivating everyday intuition. Nevertheless, even veteran mystics have been conditioned to believe that objective reasoning is the only true path to knowledge. We have all acquired habits of mind that work against, and even stifle, the intuitive mind. Therefore, if you want help from intuition in navigating the spiritual path, you have to remain alert. That means catching yourself before you suppress your intuition or dismiss an intuitive response just because, on first blush, it can't be explained. It means becoming familiar with the nuances of your own inner voice. It means allowing yourself to expect intuitive answers, to look for them, welcome them, and pay attention to them. Perhaps most of all, it means creating the right conditions for them.

Intuition is, by definition, spontaneous and usually unexpected. It's not like going to the shelf for a reference book or turning on a calculator. Intuitive thoughts and feelings come when they are ready; you can no more coerce them into being than you can force someone to fall in love with you. You can, however, make yourself available. As Shakespeare said, through Hamlet, "The readiness is all."

TRAVEL TIPS

1. *Open a space in your mind.* The best welcome mat for intuition is a mind that is quiet, calm, and spacious. Adopt habits and practices that reduce noise, agitation, and stress.

2. *Feed it raw material.* Give your subconscious plenty of information to work with. But don't stifle it with a predictable diet. Go beyond the obvious sources. Approach situations with a playful, flexible attitude and constantly question your own assumptions.

3. *Issue an invitation.* Frame the question you're pondering, and send it out to a source of higher intelligence with which you are comfortable: God, a holy figure such as Jesus or Buddha, a revered teacher, an ancestor, an angel, a formless image such as a field of light, or simply "the universe." You can write it down, speak it out, think it, or pray it. Then let it go, expecting nothing and resisting nothing.

4. *Get away from it all.* Research shows that incubation—a period of time when you're disengaged from the problem you're trying to solve—plays an important role in creativity and invention. Stop obsessing. Go somewhere and do something else.

5. *Open the cage.* Unrestricted self-expression can coax intuition to come in out of the cold. Have brainstorming sessions with others or yourself. Write freestyle, without censoring, editing, or trying to make sense. Sing, dance, or paint on the theme of whatever is bugging you. By giving voice to your subconscious you might unearth some gems.

6. *Pay attention.* Intuition often leaves calling cards where they are easily overlooked: in dreams, for example, and in the meaningful coincidences that Carl Jung called synchronicity. Stay alert to the signals that are trying to break through to your awareness.

7. *Treat it with respect.* Too often we dismiss our intuitions because they seem illogical, or because they lack proof. When you

find yourself rejecting an intuitive idea without due consideration, ask yourself:

- Is it telling me something I don't want to know?
- Is it urging me to do something that entails risk?
- Am I concerned about what others might think?
- Am I afraid to be wrong or to go against the grain?

8. *Sort out the message.* Intuition can be vague and insubstan-
tial. It can come in symbols or riddles or ambiguous language.
Its meaning might have to be decoded.

9. *Illuminate your mind.* All knowledge springs from the inex-
haustible well of divine intelligence. In classic chicken-egg
fashion, intuition will help you navigate closer to that Source,
while, in turn, a strong connection to the Divine will make your
mind more receptive to intuition. Don't skimp on spiritual practices that forge that connection.

10. Contemplate these words from the Taoist sage Lao Tzu:
"Without going out of your door you can know the ways of the
world. Without peeping through your window you can see the
Way of Heaven."

4

TRAVELERS MUST CARRY INTELLECT

*Ignorance is the curse of God; knowledge is the wing
wherewith we fly to heaven.*
—Shakespeare

At a party one evening, I was introduced to a woman as the author of *The Intuitive Edge.* She threw her arms around me and gushed, "Thank you for contributing to the death of the intellect."

"What have I done?" I thought. "Did I go too far with that 'Trust your intuition' message?" I certainly had no intention of killing the intellect, mine or anyone else's. It turned out that my admirer had never actually read the book. That its title indicated a high regard for intuition was enough to convince her that I was an ally in her war against the intellect, which she considered the enemy of everything authentically human and spiritually worthy.

In some spiritual circles, reason, analysis, and logic are treated with distrust. For some, the attitude amounts to contempt, or even misology, which the dictionary defines as "hatred of reason." They treat those with analytic minds as if they were hopelessly retro, or as if they were handicapped in some way. For them the sixties adage "If

it feels good, do it," has morphed into "If it feels right, believe it." Simplistic equations—heart equals good, head
equals bad—are accepted as axioms. Do they believe that
a trickster God created us with intellects as a test—an obstacle to circumvent, as we wend our way to the higher
wisdom of the heart? I'm with Galileo: "I do not feel
obliged to believe that the same God who has endowed us
with sense, reason, and intellect has intended us to forgo
their use."

If anything is worth killing, it is not the intellect but
the either/or thinking that turns reason and intuition into
antagonists. The mind serves us best when it shifts fluidly,
like an automatic transmission, between its various functions. Reason and analysis feed raw material to the unconscious, where it is processed into hunches and flashes
of insight. The intellect helps us evaluate those inspira-
tions. Intuition, in turn, serves the rational process by
soaring to innovative ideas that would not be possible
within the rules of logic.

> My experience is that most people who think they
> are beyond the intellect actually haven't quite gotten up
> to it yet.
> —Ken Wilber

There are excellent reasons why spiritual seekers
ought to be wary of what my Chinese acupuncturist calls
"too much brain." You don't have to search very hard in
the reputable texts to find warnings about excessive
thinking and the futility of book learning. "How much
more foolish are those who depend upon words and seek
understanding by their intellect," said Zen master Wu-
men. "They try to hit the moon with a stick. They scratch

their shoes when their feet itch." Shankara, the great reformer and exponent of Advaita Vedanta, asserted that "the Scriptures consisting of many words are a dense forest which merely causes the mind to wander in it." The 20th-century master Sri Aurobindo summed it up this way: "Mind has to cease to be mind and become brilliant with something beyond it."

Caution about the intellect runs through the Abrahamic religions as well. The Sufi mystic Mahmud Shabistari wrote, "If God guides you not into the road, it will not be disclosed by logic. Logic is a bondage of forms; a road that is long and hard." In the Book of Zohar, the central text of Kabbalah, it is written that "God conceals himself from the mind of man, but reveals himself to his heart." Even the great scholar-theologian St. Thomas Aquinas, after having written 60 books, had such a powerful experience of the Divine that he declared, "I can do no more. Such secrets have been revealed to me that all I have written now appears to be of little value."

At best, the intellect can take you to the door of the Holy; it cannot take you across the threshold. For that the mind itself must be transcended. Only in the cessation of thought can the Ultimate be encountered. Only in the shift from busy thinking to quiet feeling can love, devotion, reverence, and other qualities associated with spiritual awakening be accessed. The wise ones chuckle at our vain attempts to find realization by gorging on books and ruminating about enlightenment. They compare it to eating the menu instead of the meal or confusing the finger pointing to the moon for the moon itself. They are telling us not to get so hung up with maps, itineraries, and travel guides that we never hit the road.

Through wisdom a house is built, and by under-standing it is established.
  —Proverbs 24:3

It often comes as a great relief to learn that the mind can be a spiritual distraction and that analytic thought can be a liability. It allows us to give our brains a rest from in-cessant wheel spinning. It gives us permission to not know everything and to not have to answer the unanswerable. We love hearing stories like the one about the Zen master who, before dying, told her son in a note: "There are eighty thousand books on Buddhism, and if you should read all of them and still not see your own nature, you will not understand even this letter."

But of course I read that in one of those 80,000 books. Buddha himself famously advised his followers: "Without melting, beating, weighing, and polishing a yellow substance, one should not take it for gold. Like-wise, without analysis one should not accept the dharma[1] as valid." And Shankara, who we just heard disparage the reading of scriptures, also wrote voluminous commen-taries on those very scriptures. Indeed many of the same luminaries who have alerted us to the limitations of study and the futility of analytic thought have also extolled the *virtues* of study and analytic thought. Some of them have labored mightily to produce treatises and to interpret and reinterpret texts, not for the fun of it but because knowl-edge has value and intellectual clarity has value, just as menus have value and fingers pointing to the moon have value. "You can get something from a book," said the

---

[1] *Dharma* in this context is synonymous with Buddhist teachings.

Sufi scholar Idries Shah. "That something may be so important as to lead you to the recognition of the real thing."

If that were not the case, then all the commentaries on the Vedas, all the exegeses of the Bible, all of the Talmud and the Hadith, all the discourses by sages and pundits, all the 80 times 80,000 books on religion and spirituality—all would be colossal wastes of time. And they can be. But at the same time, they're not.

Recently, a devoted practitioner of meditation lectured me about the hazards of the intellect. With great authority and the precision of a practiced debater, he explained how the analytical mind misleads us, how it fosters illusions and gets in the way of spiritual experience. He spoke derisively about "filling one's head with ideas and concepts." All this, of course, in a well-reasoned argument, articulated with the ardor of a trial lawyer by a clear, penetrating intellect that had garnered elegant ideas through meticulous study. It was a perfect illustration of a great irony: Without a discerning intellect, we might not even know that our spiritual goals are beyond the reach of the intellect.

Of course, there are times when hitting the off switch on the thinking machine is a necessity: in meditation; when you want to be fully open to a sensory or aesthetic experience; when the mind is overtaxed or has met its match; when you remember that the divine Presence is at hand in every moment and you want to let it in. But there are other times when the intellect is an indispensable tool, such as when you have to solve a problem or make a practical decision or ferret out the truth from a lie. It makes no more sense to turn away from reason because it can't reveal the Ultimate Truth than it does to throw out hammers because they can't turn screws.

> *Study, even though you forget, even though you don't understand.*
> —*The Talmud*

We need the intellect as a watchdog at the gates of the subconscious to guard against sabotage from our emotional demons. We need it in the spiritual marketplace, or else we might consume too much of what one teacher called "gum drop metaphysics"—sweet, comforting bromides filled with the spiritual equivalent of empty calories—and fall asleep at the wheel. We need it to separate reliable information from trash; to correct misconceptions; to protect ourselves from hogwash, charlatans, and misguided teachings, not to mention our own biases.

Perhaps most of all, the intellect can help us understand our own experiences. Spiritual transformation can be sweet and glorious, but also bewildering and sometimes frightening. In his classic study of religious experience *The Idea of the Holy*, Rudolf Otto said that the *mysterium tremendum* can be "a gentle tide, pervading the mind with a tranquil mood of deepest worship." But it can also "burst in sudden eruption up from the depths of the soul with spasms and convulsions, or lead to the strangest excitements, to intoxicated frenzy, to transport, and to ecstasy. It has wild and demonic forms and can sink to an almost grisly horror and shuddering."

Without discernment, an experience as valuable as a diamond might be discarded as a piece of glass—or the opposite: A worthless rock might be placed on an altar as if it were a sacred gem. During a spiritual practice, you might, for example, encounter strange bodily sensations: Are you being blessed by purification and healing, or should you call a doctor? Along the path, you might go through mood swings: Are they a prelude to a leap forward, or should you see a therapist? Is the explosion of elation a sign of God-intoxication or a manic episode? Is your sudden lack of concern about your career a sign of healthy detachment and faith, or does it indicate apathy or denial?

It is not uncommon for seekers to mistake a profound spiritual breakthrough for a breakdown—and vice versa—or to dismiss an ecstatic encounter with the Divine as a delusion—and vice versa. A healthy, well-oiled intellect can help you defend against such errors.

Yes, the intellect can get in the way of spirit. Sure, piling up information is a sorry substitute for the experience of the Divine. Reading too much scripture can absolutely give you what Paramahansa Yogananda called "metaphysical indigestion." Think too much and you shut down your heart. Insist on analyzing everything and you close yourself off to the Great Mysteries and end up with a headache instead of enlightenment. But think too little and know too little and you're vulnerable to the hazards of ignorance, confusion, and naïveté.

The willing suspension of disbelief has a long tradition in the theater, where audiences are happy to trade veracity for entertainment or emotional catharsis. On the spiritual path, suspending disbelief is often regarded as an essential act of faith. In some traditions, doubt is regarded as something akin to sin—a weakness to be expunged. We are sometimes told to check our critical faculties at the door when we read scripture or listen to a teacher. These can be good strategies, but when taken too far they are fraught with peril. Being on the lookout for logical flaws, factual errors, and outright malarkey does not necessarily indicate a lack of faith; it asserts that you have faith that the truth will be revealed by a just and orderly universe. When approached with courage and intellectual honesty, doubt is not a millstone but rather a steppingstone to wisdom.

We need all the help we can get—from holy texts as well as direct experience, from our minds as well as our hearts, from reason as well as intuition. The balance point is this: We need to be discerning without becoming cynical and open without becoming gullible.

TRAVEL TIPS

1. If you find yourself inclined to accept something as true when you're not really sure, ask yourself if it's because:

- You *want* to believe it
- You *need* to believe it
- Believing it gives you hope
- You don't want to rock the boat
- Disbelief makes you feel unstable or afraid

2. When you're struggling with a spiritual dilemma or pondering a religious doctrine or philosophical concept:

- Gather information from a variety of sources
- Pay attention to opposing points of view
- Analyze facts and opinions as objectively as possible
- Try to test your hypothesis
- Evaluate the results as dispassionately as possible

3. *Examine your assumptions.* Write down the bedrock beliefs that underpin your approach to spirituality. About each one, ask yourself:

- How do I know this?
- What is this assumption based on?
- How can I be sure it's true?
- Has it been put to the test?
- Have I considered opposing ideas?

4. *Read deeply.* Scriptures and commentaries are multilayered gifts whose value increases with each level of meaning you unveil. Bear in mind that most great works have been translated and interpreted many times over. Consider the context in which it originated and contemplate what the original intent might have been. When reading religious stories, don't just take them literally, as history, but also metaphorically: What might the

characters and plot points symbolize? Can they stand for processes that unfold inwardly, in the landscape of the mind and spirit?

5. *Use your head, but don't be fooled by it.* The intellect is a tricky devil: It will try to delude you into thinking that understanding is the same as knowing and that intellectual insight is the same as realization. They are not.

6. Contemplate this statement from the scholar of religion Huston Smith: "The larger the island of knowledge, the longer the shoreline of mystery." Ponder as well Smith's distinction between two types of unknowns: the unknown we know we don't know and "the unknown we don't know we don't know until we advance and find out what more we don't know."

5

MERGE WITH OTHERS

Come, let us grow together.
—Rig-Veda

While the true workplace for spiritual aspirants is in the private smithy of the soul, there are blessings to be had in companionship. It is not for nothing that every tradition calls its followers together in a community of spiritual brethren.

Without trusted, respected, accessible comrades, where will you find protection, comfort, and support when life on the path gets difficult? Who will ask penetrating questions that force you to dig ever deeper for self-understanding? With whom will you share the upsurge of love, the unspeakable bliss, the mighty insights that spring like fountains from your spiritual practices? Where will you find solace when you can't reconcile your current despair with the ecstasy you knew a week ago? Where will you turn for a second opinion when you're tempted to join a monastery? Who will bust you when you veer off track or get spiritually lazy?

It is said that in ancient China, warriors carried swords of such length that they were impossible to unsheathe when the scabbard was worn. This ensured that the warriors would travel in pairs; in times of trouble, they could draw each other's swords. Spiritual companions can provide an analogous service. When the demons of doubt and confusion snap at your heels, forcing you to lose sight of your values or slack off on your practices, like-thinking friends can rekindle your spiritual passion and reinforce your tenuous convictions. When you think you're nuts for devoting time and resources to such an amorphous pursuit as divine union; when the teaching that hit you like a bolt of pure truth starts to sound like sugarcoated drivel; when you think you're getting nowhere fast; when you're disillusioned by spiritual stalwarts who display the foibles of ordinary human beings; when you start to think the path is a treadmill paved in rubbish and you're ready to cut your losses and run—at such times, trusted companions can hold you steady and bolster your faith. And if your friends are as concerned with your truth as they are your comfort, they will also, at times, puncture your safe assumptions, shatter your illusions, and turn your self-serving logic on its ear.

Companions are also essential when you're trying to make sense of thoughts, perceptions, and feelings that defy your preconceptions, or when you stumble into an experience for which you have no frame of reference. They can offer cogent explanations, packaged in a shared language and wrapped in empathy. The range of potential experiences on any spiritual path is vast, and they don't come in any predictable order. Chances are, someone in your circle will already have gone through what you're now going through. Someone has probably read something you have not, remembers something you don't, or has had an insight that has so far eluded you.

Take, for instance, a novice mediator named Jean who

began to feel separate from her body. Watching her flesh move through space as though on a movie screen and hearing words emanate from her mouth as if from a loudspeaker was disorienting, even though accompanied by a sense of delight more enchanting than anything she'd known before. A therapist gave the condition a clinical label and spoke so gravely that Jean became terrified. Fortunately, she also mentioned it to a friend, who gave her some reputable literature on mystical experience. She came to realize that she was having a protracted experience of a most welcome state that yogis call *sahaj samadhi* or witnessing—pure, undiluted consciousness along with normal sense impressions.

> *Because there is one bread, we who are many are one body, for we all partake of the one bread.*
> —1 Corinthians 10:18–19

True camaraderie can speed the progress of every member, but only if you choose your companions well, and only if you avoid dysfunctions such as competitiveness and insular thinking, which afflict many spiritual groups. It is also important to guard against becoming overly dependent on your buddies or replicating through peer pressure the conformity that has turned so many away from established institutions. "There is a dangerous tendency to lean on one another as we tread the path," wrote Trungpa Rinpoche in *Cutting Through Spiritual Materialism*. "If a group of people leans one upon the other, then if one should happen to fall down, everyone falls down. So we do not lean on anyone else. We just walk with each other, side by side, shoulder to shoulder, working with each other, going with each other."

Here are some of the qualities of a good spiritual friend. He or she:

- Genuinely cares about your spiritual development
- Listens deeply, with the heart as well as the mind
- Helps you comprehend your own thoughts, feelings, and perceptions
- Challenges your assumptions
- Reinforces your truth and ruthlessly—but kindly—reveals your self-deceptions
- Urges you to delve deeper, deeper, and still deeper for truth
- Shares useful tools, resources, and information
- Wants to know what you know and hear what you need to say
- Helps you find spiritual lessons in life's ups and downs
- Is worthy of your trust
- Walks his or her talk and helps you walk yours
- Bolsters your courage when you falter

That list will not only help you choose the best companions, it will help you *be* the best companion. If you think you don't need support because you are the spiritual equivalent of the High Plains Drifter, consider this: Somewhere, some pilgrim needs comfort, support, feedback, and insight. You may be able to give it. And that may be the best reason to join forces with others. The opportunity to serve your fellow seekers can be of greater spiritual value than anything you can hope to receive from them.

I am because we are. We are because I am.
—African saying

For independent travelers, companionship can be a catch-as-catch-can proposition. One way to lend it regularity is to round up some spiritual chums and form a support group of your own. Here are some issues that you and your companions will have to consider.

Diversity or uniformity?

Cozy groups consisting of people on the same path offer common terminology, beliefs, rituals, and practices. Diverse groups, on the other hand, can be exciting crucibles in which ideas from varied sources can mingle.

What is the main purpose?

Do you want to be a support group that stresses emotional comfort? A discussion group, where a dialogue of ideas is the focus? A reading group that studies sacred literature? A religious group that emphasizes inspiration and ritual?

Should there be a format?

Do you want every session to revolve around a theme or cover items on a set agenda? If so, how will they be selected? Should discussion be free-form or follow a formal procedure? Shall there be an opening and/or closing ritual, and if so, will it vary or will it always be the same?

Are there rules?

Which rules, if any, would best serve the purposes of your group? Many gatherings, for example, insist that everything said in meetings be kept confidential.

Should there be a leader?

If so, does the same person lead each session, or do the members alternate that responsibility? What authority shall the leader be granted, and exactly what role is he or she expected to play?

How often should your group meet?

With frequency you get greater continuity and intimacy, but also more absenteeism. Is once a week too often? Is once a month or bimonthly too infrequent?

How big should your group be?

Too small and the meetings can bog down in familiarity and repetition; too big and they can lack intimacy or become unwieldy. Too small and you might lack diversity; too big and you might lack coherence.

Should you add members?

The occasional introduction of fresh blood can keep a group lively and prevent spiritual inbreeding. But if you make the wrong choices, it can spoil the chemistry.

How should you deal with difficult issues?

Don't assume that because your gang consists of highly aware souls that tensions will never crop up. Try to agree from the get-go how you will manage disagreements and conflicts. You might, for example, agree that each member will take responsibility for resolving issues in a way that supports everyone's spiritual growth.

TRAVEL TIPS

1. On a scale of one to five, using the criteria in this chapter, how would you rate your current spiritual companions?

2. List the most important qualities you would like your spiritual friends to have.

3. If you would like to be part of a community whose members meet those criteria, how can you find one—or create one?

4. On a scale of one to five, how would you rate yourself as a spiritual friend?

5. List the qualities you wish to cultivate to become a better companion to others.

6. Contemplate this parable from the Jewish tradition: A man has been wandering in the forest for several days unable to find the way out. Finally, he sees another man approaching him, looking weary and worn. Elated, he asks the traveler to show him how to get home. The man replies, "I have been wandering for many days, unable to find the way out. I can tell you that it is not in the direction I have come from. So let us search for the way together."

6

POSSIBLE DELAYS DUE TO ORGANIZED TOURS

Would to God that religions multiplied
until every man had his own religion,
quite separate from that of any other.
—*Swami Vivekananda*

The joke is told that a couple of thousand years ago, Satan's emissaries told their boss that a big problem was brewing on earth. "It seems there's this rabbi from Nazareth," they reported. "So far he has only twelve disciples, but he's getting more and more popular, and it looks like he could be trouble."

"No problem," says Satan. "If he gathers more followers he'll have to organize, and then we'll be fine."

Spiritual institutions have a mixed reputation because most of us have had mixed experiences with them. This should not be surprising, since all organizations reflect—and in some respects magnify—the strengths and weaknesses of the human beings that make up their constituencies. And how we respond to institutions reflects our *own* strengths and weaknesses.

My personal experience has been typical in many ways: I started out antagonistic to organized religion, got deeply involved with an unconventional spiritual institution, pulled away in disappointment, and have since kept my distance while also mellowing toward organizations in general. The intimate, inspiring, but imperfect community in which I dwelled for a number of years has my gratitude for getting my journey off to a good start. It was not only a true sanctuary, but it enabled me to solidify my spiritual commitment, master a number of powerful practices, learn incalculable lessons, and acquire a way of looking at life that has, for the most part, endured.

At the time (the late '60s to mid-'70s), there were plenty of other spiritual institutions on the landscape, both traditional Western brands and imports, with brilliant leaders and splendid teachings. But many of them demanded a level of conformity with which I was uncomfortable. The Transcendental Meditation organization appealed to me largely because it was pragmatic and relatively free of rules and cultlike trappings. As with any formal group, there was a certain amount of self-created peer pressure, and those who represented the organization in public, as I did, were required to toe certain lines, such as cleaning up one's appearance. But, in general, I felt less pressure to conform than I would have had I gone to work for the average corporation, and I resented it a whole lot less. I was never ostracized for my occasional irreverence, and my impertinent questions were tolerated by most of the people who mattered. The central credo was basically "Meditate and live your life," not "Follow me" or "Do as I say." It also mattered that I could walk away any time I chose without some Gestapo trying to bar the exit.

Nevertheless, at a certain point I had to pull away.

The community in which I had thrived began to grow

progressively more rigid, conformist, and exclusionary—
or perhaps it had always been that way and it took some
time and maturation before I could see it. Most likely it
was some combination of the two. In any case, I eventually came to feel insulated and constrained. Like a student
graduating from college, I packed up the treasures I'd acquired during my stay, tossed out what no longer served
me, and, with a mix of relief and regret, ventured forth to
the "real world."

Disengaging from the group enabled me to mature
psychologically and grow spiritually in ways I could not
have otherwise. Still, as the years passed, I would often
feel that something was missing. I missed the sense of
family, the intellectual and emotional camaraderie, the be-
longing.

> *The community is created, not when people come*
> *together in the name of religion, but when they come*
> *together bringing honesty, respect, and kindness to*
> *support an awakening of the sacred.*
> —*Jack Kornfield*

The path I traversed—plunging into an exclusive affiliation and then becoming more autonomous—is a venerable
pattern. Like young trees that need to be encircled by a protective fence until they are strong enough to keep from
being knocked over, spiritual neophytes often need the security of an enclosed organization until they're mature
enough to wander safely outside the borders. Another
common pattern is to begin with a period of wide-ranging
exploration and to follow that with a strong institutional
commitment. This is analogous to young men and women
who date a variety of people before committing to a mate.

In recent years, a third pattern has emerged: fluctuating between periods of affiliation and independence—joining and leaving again and again in the equivalent of serial monogamy. As with relationships, the value of this pattern depends on what each individual brings to the arrangement.

Americans are ambivalent joiners. We respect those who sacrifice for a larger good and celebrate those who perform their duties without reservation. But we also view compliance with institutional power as a weakness rather than a virtue. We value loyalty, but we also prize the skillful pursuit of self-interest, and we're leery of anything that smacks of follow-the-leader. We honor fidelity, but we celebrate free spirits and we richly reward entrepreneurs, free agent athletes, and company-hopping executives. Our founding fathers were rebels, after all, and one of our most potent archetypes is the lone cowboy, rugged and solitary, riding the range with a compass all his own. "I Gotta Be Me" is our anthem, "Question Authority" our national bumper sticker.

All for good reason. If you relinquish your judgment to groupthink or the caprices of an authority figure, you can easily lose touch with your uniqueness and betray your deepest values. In many spiritual organizations, even mildly dissenting opinions are discouraged, if not forbidden, and those who ask penetrating questions are ostracized. Often this is justified in the name of sheltering the innocent from doubt and confusion. But seekers have as much responsibility to ask tough questions as they do to listen. Suppressed doubt usually leads to one of two extremes: fanaticism or rebellion. Sometimes one follows the other in rapid succession.

Another hazard of membership is the group pressure

that often leads individuals to make inappropriate choices. The institutional culture can also foster "spiritual materialism," with members competing for the attention of leaders, making ostentatious displays of their piety, or angling for the inside track: "I must attend every service/take every workshop/have every initiation/join every committee, or else . . . or else . . . I'll fall behind!" I've known people who made life-altering decisions—dropped out of school, quit jobs, rejected medical advice, walked out of marriages—because they were lured by an organization's promise of celestial nectar, only to end up broke, behind, bedridden, or bereft and still decidedly unenlightened.

Organizations can also promote self-importance—the tendency for members to think they're among the Chosen. Maybe even one of the Elect among the Chosen. The obvious hazard in this is ego inflation. But there are others as well. For example, to reinforce that they are, indeed, special, the group acts as if everything is hunky-dory even if it isn't. This keeps members from recognizing where they need to grow and prevents the attainment of a crucial realization: We're all unique emanations of the Divine and at the same time profoundly and irreversibly ordinary. Also, if your group is chosen, then everyone else is *not* chosen, which creates a huge chasm between you and all those presumably lost souls out there.

Of course, spiritual institutions are also notorious for producing the opposite of self-importance: self-flagellation. While a certain amount of ego deflation is good for the soul, spiritual inadequacy is toxic. Red flags should go up if your mental chatter starts to include thoughts like, "What's wrong with me? Why don't I feel

DON'T THROW OUT
THE BABY
WITH THE BATHWATER

One of my fondest memories of the years I spent in the TM organization is knowing the late entertainer Andy Kaufman. Andy had a provision in his employment contracts guaranteeing him time to meditate. Whenever possible, he would go on long retreats. Then his career took on the outrageous twist of wrestling women, and a TM official told him he was no longer welcome. Andy remained bitter about it for the rest of his tragically curtailed life.

But he kept on meditating. His daily practice was a sanctuary of peace and strength in his losing battle with cancer.

Not everyone who cuts the cord to a spiritual group makes the crucial distinction between the institution and the teaching and between the personalities and the practices. In contrast to Andy, consider Sharon, a devoted follower of a well-known teacher. As she moved up the organizational ladder, closer to the top where the leader resided in splendor

what the others feel? Why don't I get it? Why does the priest/minister/rabbi/guru like her better than me? I must be unevolved/a hopeless sinner/spiritually retarded."

> *Where it is a duty to worship the sun, it is pretty sure to be a crime to examine the laws of heat.*
> —*John Morley*

Having said all that, this too must be said: Despite the shortcomings of formal organizations, seekers who keep their wits about them are often very well served by joining one. Think of them as packaged tours. They can be sti-

like the angel atop a Christmas tree, the demands on her intensified. When she complained that her duties made it impossible to do her spiritual practices, she was told, "Work *is* your practice." She had no contact with the outside world, and, since romantic entanglements were forbidden, she lost the man she still considers, longingly, the love of her life.

Eventually, feeling oppressed, lonely, and burned out, she left. She was so bitter that for nearly two decades she renounced everything spiritual, like a betrayed spouse who scorns the institution of marriage.

Virtually everyone who associates with an organization discovers something he or she does not like. You can accept the flaws and remain where you are; participate but maintain some psychic distance; leap like an electron to an orbit far from the nucleus; or chuck the affiliation altogether. What's vital in any case is to separate what is useful from what is not, what is beneficial from what is harmful, what serves your needs and values from what betrays them. The ability to make such distinctions can, to a large extent, determine your spiritual progress.

fling, inhibiting, irritating, and restrictive. They can waste your time with useless activities and keep you from seeing the most sparkling treasures. But they can also make a journey safer, more comfortable, and in many ways more practical, and they can lend order and focus to your itinerary. Among the potential rewards are community, discipline, tradition, theological and moral consistency, personal guidance, and mutual support. They are yours to be had—*if* you find an affiliation that suits your needs, your personality, and your ethical standards; *if* you can remain true to your personality and values; and *if* you can tolerate the follies that afflict most organizations. Because they mirror their all-too-human members, even the most seemingly ideal institutions contain a certain amount of rigidity, dogmatism, conformity, competition, bureaucratic farce, and dubious policies. So if you are determined to remain a lonesome cowpoke until you find the perfect organization, you'll end up living the Groucho Marx joke about his not wanting to join a club that would have him as a member.

Fortunately, affiliation does not have to be an all-or-nothing proposition. Almost all spiritual organizations allow for varying degrees of involvement, with each deepening level representing an orbit closer to the nucleus, where the power resides. It is often assumed that the closer you get to the core the more access you'll have to grace, wisdom, and spiritual opportunity. To some extent, that might be true. But you have to be able to stand the heat. The further in you go, the more demands will be made on your time, loyalty, and individuality. You're also more likely to run into the kind of personalities that give spiritual organizations a bad name: callous bureaucrats; power-loving tyrants; sharp-elbowed followers battling for attention; robots who are incapable of thinking for themselves.

On the other hand, if you find a good match, you will also meet decent, humble, kind-hearted souls who are doing their best to advance spiritually and also be of service. You may meet people who are so pure, so loving, so free of egotism and guile that they appear to be candidates for sainthood. You may find companions who can be your sacred buddies for the rest of your life.

God requires no synagogue except in the heart.
—*Hasidic saying*

Strictly speaking, no one seeking the peace that surpasses understanding really needs the trappings of an organization—not the buildings, not the rituals, not the
anointed leaders, not the fellowship—because the true
abode of the Divine is in the heart. Alan Watts once said,
"The religious attitude appropriate to our time is not one
of clinging to rocks but of learning how to swim." Nevertheless, a spiritual organization that fits you well can
help you develop the strength and skill to swim on your
own. And every swimmer needs a rock to cling to while
getting used to the water or when the seas of the soul get
rough and you're pummeled by the waves of karma. At
the right time and place, therefore, a formal institution
might be just the rock you need. Just keep your eyes open
and a life jacket at the ready.

TRAVEL TIPS

1. If you're involved with a spiritual organization, these questions can help you determine the level of engagement that's best for you:

- Can you really be yourself, or do you feel like a phony?
- Is there pressure to conform in thought or behavior?
- Do any policies or practices violate your personal ethics?
- Are the members fanatical?
- Are you expected to give more money, time, or energy than seems appropriate?
- Over time, do members become more grounded or more spaced-out? More self-reliant or more dependent?
- Are "outsiders" considered inferior?
- Are the leaders arrogant or self-important?
- Is constructive criticism discouraged or punished?
- Can the members laugh at themselves?
- When someone is upset or troubled, is he or she patronized? Avoided like a leper? Treated with compassion? Given help?
- Is it taboo to discuss certain topics or raise certain issues?
- Is the public face at odds with what you see on the inside?

2. A critical factor in the long-term health of an organization is how honestly it conducts self-assessments and how effectively it self-corrects. When something goes wrong or a serious flaw is exposed, do the leaders:

- Cover it up?
- Spin it to make them or the institution look good?
- Deal with the issue openly and honestly?
- Use it as an opportunity to improve the organizational culture?

3. There might be pressure to conform or to surrender your will. You have to find your personal comfort zone between trust in yourself and trust in the institution. Constantly monitor yourself to see if you are letting go or holding on for the right reasons.

4. Contemplate this poem by the 12th-century Muslim mystic Ibn Arabi: "There was a time when I blamed my companion if his religion did not resemble mine / Now, however, my heart accepts every form: it is pasture ground for gazelles, a cloister for monks / A temple for idols and a *Ka'bah* for the pilgrim, thy tables of the Torah and the sacred books of the Koran / Love alone is my religion, and wherever their beasts of burden go, there is my religion and my faith."

7

WARNING: GUIDES ARE NOT LICENSED

A teacher affects eternity;
he can never tell where his influence stops.
—Henry Adams

Few things are more ambiguous on the spiritual path than the role of authority figures. From our teachers we acquire knowledge; we learn spiritual disciplines; we connect to sacred traditions and receive the wisdom of the ancients; we're instructed in esoteric rituals; we gain moral and ethical guidance; and, if we're lucky, we receive personal spiritual direction. In some cases we also gain role models who inspire us to drive on toward the Divine. Historically, most people had little or no opportunity to select their own teacher; they were stuck with the parish priest, the village shaman, the local rabbi or minister. We, on the other hand, have an enormous variety to choose from. The price for that opportunity is personal vigilance.

Whether it's an ordained cleric at a worship service or a self-made guru at a workshop, each of us has to decide how much we are willing to trust that person. Trust too little and we shut out vital knowledge; trust too much and we can end up misled, exploited, or even abused.

Every tradition asks for a certain amount of deference to its representatives. How much, of course, varies widely. On one end of the spectrum, the spiritual leader is considered first among equals and submission amounts to little more than giving him or her the benefit of the doubt about the tenets of a faith. On the other end, the teacher is revered as an intermediary between humans and the Divine, or even as an incarnation of God. At that extreme, trust can amount to total submission to someone presumed to be infallible. In our culture, that form of discipleship has historically been found only in isolated sects and offbeat cults. It became more widespread, however, when the Eastern model arrived on our shores along with teachers who attracted a high degree of devotion. The "guru system," as it has been called, has touched a surprisingly large number of seekers over the past few decades, and it serves as a cautionary model for our relationship with *all* spiritual authorities.

> *A teacher should have maximal authority, and minimal power.*
> —*Thomas Szasz*

I was not a very good disciple myself. In the years I followed Maharishi Mahesh Yogi, I looked up to him, I was grateful to him, I felt honored to serve him. But I did not, *could* not, worship him or think of him as infallible. I cherished my time with him, but I had little desire to be among the privileged that buzzed around him all the time. I trusted what he said about meditation, consciousness, and other subjects on which he was an authority, but I questioned his judgment on other issues. And I could never bring myself to do everything he said to do.

Once, at the end of a long retreat, I was confused about what work to take on when I returned to the United States. Why not just ask him? I thought. As an enlightened master he presumably knows me better than I know myself. Others asked him what to do all the time. In fact, at that very moment, they were queuing up by the dozen to do just that. I hopped into line. I felt relieved to be turning over a pressing issue to an awareness greater than my own. And then, with only two people between me and my goal, I suddenly bolted from the room. *What if he tells me something I don't want to hear?* The very idea made me panic.

I was convinced that I was spiritually retarded. I assumed that those who could surrender their will to a master had an evolutionary advantage—the spiritual equivalent of opposable thumbs. Surely they would be floating in the bliss of enlightenment while I was still wallowing in the mud of self-absorbed ignorance. I hoped to become a better disciple one day, when my ego evaporated and I got over my knee-jerk resistance to authority.

Eventually, I came to see my resistance as a fortunate trait. It kept me from becoming overly dependent. As for those I'd envied, I learned that for every humble devotee who had surrendered in selfless service, there were fifty who were faking it, forcing it, trying it on for size, desperately seeking a parent figure, or infatuated like giddy teenagers in the grip of a first crush. When they discovered signs that their master was human, many were consumed by indignation, and when it was time to leave the womb, many had difficulty adjusting.

I have since met many other teachers, from local pastors to celebrity gurus. Some were radiant with love and redolent with wisdom. I am inspired by them. I am grateful to be in their presence. I will happily offer them every sign of respect. I will donate to their causes. I will be a sponge for their wisdom. But I can't prostrate myself before them or worship them. I can't hang on their every word as if they were all-knowing. I can't trust them without reservation as if they were beyond human frailty. It is just not my way.

I have to admit that my early experience has left me somewhat jaded. When I am in the company of followers who are giddy with adoration for a teacher, I find myself squirming. When they coo over every adorable gesture, sigh at every clever remark, and blabber on about how magnificent he or she is—well, I confess to a certain instinct to expel the rude sound that used to be called the raspberry. The more they gush the more uncomfortable I get, because inherent in their song of praise is an invitation for me to join in, like the beckoning of a wedding singer who thinks you'll have the time of your life if only you'd get out there on the dance floor.

I find myself thinking, What is their problem? Why are these smart people so willing to suspend their critical faculties? Afterward, however, I often reflect back on the encounter and think, Who am I to judge? Maybe it's *my* problem. The ways of another's heart are beyond comprehension. Isn't it wonderful that they can love someone, *anyone,* with such fervor? Is that not a rare and precious thing and, therefore, to be admired and respected?

It is indeed rare and precious—when it's real. When I see the genuine, unforced love of a devoted student, it is like watching tender old spouses holding hands on a park bench or the joy in the faces of children when they see their parents. It can be that pure, that beautiful, that miraculous. But when it feels like a contrivance I find it insufferable. I'm not proud of this, but I can't help it.

And yet, every once in a while, I wonder if I am not missing out on something.

> *The true teacher defends his pupils against his own personal influence. He inspires self-distrust. He guides their eyes from himself to the spirit that quickens him.*
>
> —*Amos Bronson Alcott*

In a culture where the attitude toward authority is cheeky at best, it is easy to dismiss all spiritual obedience as weakness, gullibility, or fear. But that is much too facile. For one thing, surrender in some instances is an act of strength that, when properly managed, can yield sublime spiritual rewards. For another, we all have to defer to experts, whether they're accountants, electricians, scientists, or the clergy. Spiritual trust, therefore, might arise from something central to the American character: consumer-like pragmatism. Teachers represent the promise of grace, and the best of them embody it in such a way that we want what they're selling. Teachers have been compared to skilled navigators who guide the ignorant to hidden treasures; to parents who show children how to tie their shoelaces; to oarsmen who ferry travelers to the other shore; and countless other metaphors suggesting the need for expert help. The risk comes when we go beyond trust in another's expertise and relinquish our judgment and will.

Surrender appeals to many because a lot more than

FOLLOW THE FOLLOWERS

A worthy teacher will produce admirable students. If you're evaluating a prospective teacher, see what the long-term students are like. See how they treat one another, how grounded they are, and how mature they are. Look out for signs of spiritual dependency.

- *Personality cult.* Is the teacher considered infallible or immune to normal standards of morality? Are banal remarks taken to be revelations and odd behavior considered brilliant teaching tools?

- *The halo effect.* It's one thing to defer to qualified teachers on spiritual matters and quite another to grant them authority in other areas of life. Don't assume that their expertise is infinite.

---

guidance and knowledge is promised to those who accept the challenge. This assumes certain things: that the anointed have reached the highest levels of attainment; that devotion to such teachers is necessary to reach the same heights; and that the proper attitude to bring to the relationship is one of obedience. This outlook is encapsulated in this passage from a Hindu text: "The Guru is the Spiritual Father of the disciple; he takes the disciple in his own being, fills him with consciousness, links the destiny of the novice with his own, and thus makes him a permanent part of himself. The disciple surrenders to him wholly, and his well-being and progress depend upon his faithfulness to the Guru who is carrying him on the path." Strains of all religions call upon aspirants to become vessels for the holy ones to fill. John of the Cross declared

- *Ipse dixit.* That's what followers of Pythagoras would say when they wanted to settle an argument. It means, "He said it." Be careful if a teacher's word is considered the final reference point for truth.
- *Alleged powers.* No doubt some spiritual masters have supernormal abilities. But watch out for the *assumption* of it on the part of followers.
- *My guru can lick your guru.* I once was present when Maharishi met with Swami Muktananda. After the summit meeting, the buzz was that Maharishi dwarfed his companion in stature and wisdom. Later, I found out that Muktananda's followers said the same exact thing about him. Be careful when students claim that their teacher is the one, the only, the best.

that "The soul which has virtue but remains on its own without a Master is like a burning coal which is left to itself; it loses its glow and grows cold."

A subtle alchemy is said to take place when the student's will is attuned to that of the teacher. This presumably occurs through the transmission of spiritual energy—something analogous to an orchestral musician tuning an instrument to the first violin. Even more alluring, the devotion and love for a venerated teacher is said to be transferable, like a deed, to God, resulting in the highest levels of grace.

For many seekers, this sounds too enticing to resist, but it is also demanding and inherently risky. Tibetans compare gurus to fire: Stay too far away and you don't get warm; get too close and you can get burned. Teachers have also been compared to master craftsmen whose task is to mold the unformed clay of the student. But how do you know you won't end up in the hands of a fraud who will turn you into an ashtray instead of a masterpiece?

A number of commentators have denounced the master-disciple model as archaic and inherently oppressive. We have divested mainstream priests and ministers of absolute authority, they argue, so why hand it to the imports and the self-anointed? Others disagree, and some even claim that the highest rungs of development can only be reached through a fully realized master. Mata Amritanandamayi (Ammachi), one of the more beloved of contemporary gurus, says that obedience is absolutely necessary to rise to the spiritual heights. "If teachers are indispensable in ordinary life," she reasons, "wouldn't we need a teacher even more on the spiritual path, which is so extremely subtle?"

Ah, but Ammachi herself did not have a personal master. En route to whatever state of consciousness she's attained, she considered "the whole of creation" her guru. Do what she says, or do what she did? It depends.

> *If you bow at all, bow low.*
> —*Chinese proverb*

The legendary 19th-century sage Ramakrishna said that "He who can himself approach God with sincerity, earnest prayer, and deep longing needs no Guru." He added that such people are rare. But in the West the spirit of a true disciple is even more rare. Even those who are not at risk for emotional, financial, or sexual exploitation feel they have to be prudent with their trust. At the same time, if we're too guarded we can build walls so high they block the light.

Ultimately, each of us is his or her own master. Whether you are a devoted follower or a dyed-in-the-wool independent, you have to assume responsibility for your own development and become, as Buddha urged his own disciples, a lamp unto yourself. If you find the right teacher at the right time, the marriage can be made in heaven. But you and you alone decide at every moment whom to trust and whom not to trust, what to follow and what to reject. Each of us has to ask ourselves: What kind of help do I need? What am I willing to do to get it? What kind of student-teacher relationship best suits my personality and my spiritual needs? "The outer teacher is merely a milestone," said Nisargadatta Maharaj. "It is only your inner teacher that will walk with you to the goal, for he is the goal."

Ah, but a good outer teacher can put you in touch with that inner sage.

TRAVEL TIPS

1. *Define the role*. Which role or roles are you most comfortable assigning to the teachers in your life?

Advisor	Friend	Master
Commander	Guide	Mentor
Companion	Instructor	Role Model
Expert	Intermediary	

2. *Choose wisely*. "Before taking someone as a teacher, be careful," the Dalai Lama advises. "Use your critical faculty and subject that teacher to scrutiny." See if the teacher's private face matches his or her public face, he adds.

3. *Hold them to high standards*. Make sure the teacher merits your trust. The path is littered with disheartened followers who thought it was improper to question the behavior of a teacher or felt that their concerns reflected their own shortcomings. What are your nonnegotiable standards?

4. *Don't expect perfection*. Standards are one thing; *realistic* standards are quite another. If you expect a teacher to be perfect, you might abandon a useful helper at the first sign of a flaw. Worse, you can fool yourself into justifying egregious behavior. Even in the light of irrefutable evidence, exploitation has been explained away as a teaching tool. Regardless of their inner attainments, spiritual teachers are still human. We get into trouble if we project onto them our fantasies of divine perfection.

5. *Hold yourself to high standards*. What we get from teachers depends on what we draw out of them. Are you inquisitive? Sincere? Disciplined? Humble? Being a good student requires unassuming openness along with honest persistence in pursuit of truth.

6. *Don't give up your will*. Unless you're a vow-taking monk or nun, taking on a teacher does not mean turning over your power. No matter how devoted you are you do not have to ab-

dicate responsibility. In Thomas Merton's perceptive commentaries on the monastic life, he says, "No one can become a saint or a contemplative merely by abandoning himself unintelligently to an oversimplified concept of obedience . . . [Obedience] implies a mature mind able to make difficult decisions."

7. *The teacher is not the teaching.* Remembering that distinction can spare you a lot of trouble. If, for example, you discover that a teacher has personal flaws, it might not mean that the teaching is wrong—not any more than Einstein's inability to keep his hair combed casts doubt on the theory of relativity.

8. *Why just one?* Even traditions in which seekers are expected to commit to a master often encourage learning from others as well, for different teachers can serve different needs. In the Mishnah, the Jewish oral tradition, it is said that anyone from whom you learn even one thing is worthy of reverence.

9. Contemplate this true story from a woman named Marcy. During a crisis in her life, Marcy turned to her spiritual teacher, who told her, "Put your faith in me completely. I will always look after you, so stop worrying and be joyful." She was greatly relieved. Some time later, in a gathering of followers, the teacher said, "You are all completely responsible for your lives."

Marcy protested: "That's the complete opposite of what you told me before."

"You're right," he replied. "And they're both one hundred percent true."

8

EXPLORE AT YOUR
OWN RISK

*A man has no religion who has not slowly and painfully
gathered one together, adding to it, shaping it.*

—D. H. Lawrence

In Paula's apartment in Santa Monica, secured by fruit-shaped magnets to the door of her refrigerator where shopping lists and take-out menus would normally be posted are menus of a different sort: event calendars for the Self-Realization Fellowship, the Agape International Spiritual Center, the Zen Center of Los Angeles, a yoga studio, and the Methodist church where she worships most Sundays. In a magazine rack sit *Tricycle*, a Buddhist magazine; *Yoga Journal*; and a copy of *The Whole Life Times*, opened to a compendium of seminars and services. Paula is an eclectic freelancer, treading a bebop path of improvisation and personal expression. She meditates here, prays there, joins in rituals, enrolls in workshops, always reaching for the light like a heat-seeking missile. Some have said that her path lacks depth and discipline. She replies that her commitment is to Truth, not to a particular teaching, tradition, or belief system.

In the land of the free and the home of the brave, what

could be more inevitable than an eclectic, experimental spirituality? The freedom to shop is almost as sacred as freedom of speech. Consumer choice is considered such a birthright that we invented antitrust laws and turned the word *monopoly* into a pejorative except when it applies to a board game. "Don't put all your eggs in one basket" is a universally accepted maxim. "Diversify" is a Wall Street mantra. Why not apply it to matters of the spirit, particularly now that millions have access to wisdom that once reached only a handful of privileged souls?

It could be argued that eclecticism goes against the grain of custom. Historically, seekers of the Divine kept to the straight and narrow path of the tradition to which they were born. Even the wisdom teachings of the East, which inform so much of today's personalized spirituality, tend to favor steadfast affiliations. Ramakrishna, for example, compared dabblers to a man who digs a number of shallow wells but never burrows deep enough to find water. Others have used different metaphors—try to catch two rabbits at the same time and you won't catch either; you can't float downstream in more than one boat—but the message is essentially the same: Choose a path and stick to it. Don't mix and match. Don't trade depth for variety. Don't be seduced by an illusory sense of freedom. As with marriage, they say, the rewards of spiritual fidelity accrue over time.

It is hard not to hear the melody of practical wisdom in that advice. A case could be made that discarding a serviceable teaching for a shiny new model is the equivalent of conspicuous consumption and that consumerism is out of place in matters of the spirit. It could be said that if you treat spiritual teachings like items at a buffet, you'll eat only what looks good and, as a consequence, end up undernourished. It might be argued that eclectics are likely to quit the minute they feel uncomfortable or frustrated, abandoning useful teachings before they've had a chance to harvest their potential. Instead of dealing constructively with difficult challenges, they might simply roam to where the grass looks greener and better manicured.

Anyone who ventures into the spiritual marketplace runs the risk of becoming a dilettante, sampling one offering after another, like a single person who goes on an endless series of first dates without really getting to know anyone. There is also the related danger of spiritual promiscuity: voraciously devouring each new workshop, teacher, or philosophy with passion, only to plunge with equal zeal into the next one, like a midnight club-hopper looking for love in all the wrong places. On either extreme, your progress might be more horizontal than vertical, and your experiences might be broader than they are deep.

There is also the risk of consumer burnout; with so many choices available, all slickly packaged with tantalizing promises, it's easy to get overwhelmed. It's also easy to get caught up in a kind of spiritual acquisitiveness in which books, seminars, and techniques pile up like clothing in the closets of compulsive shoppers. A got-to-have-it mentality can set in, aggravated by wishful thinking. Like desperate singles who imagine that every attractive person they meet is The One, seekers often see each new teaching as the possible Key to the Kingdom.

All of which makes for a strong argument against eclecticism.

A vital faith is more like an organism or a work of art than it is like a cafeteria tray.
—Huston Smith

But sometimes it makes eminently good sense to explore freely and without restraint. A stubborn commitment to a single pathway can be a hindrance to growth if it causes you to stick with something that no longer works. It can keep you at arm's length from knowledge and practices that might very well hit the spot. Sometimes, therefore, it makes practical sense to discard the old or add to it something fresh.

This exploratory approach has been denounced by many religious leaders. But the critics fail to take into account these factors: 1) religions evolve by adapting to new beliefs and customs, and even the most established traditions are internally diverse and constantly changing, and 2) the yearning for the Divine flows toward useful knowledge wherever it can be found, and in pluralistic cultures it is bound to flow widely. Like our well-stocked supermarkets, the abundance of spiritual choices can be a magnificent blessing if we make intelligent choices.

The benefits of open exploration accrue not only to eclectic freelancers but also to dedicated adherents of a single path whose minds are both open and discerning. Many shoppers in the spiritual bazaar are thoughtful, seasoned veterans. Furthermore, not every seeker who ventures beyond the familiar rejects his or her heritage. Exposure to other teachings not only increases understanding of the diversity of paths, it can also illuminate and deepen one's own.

I know dedicated Christians and Jews who took up Eastern meditative disciplines to deepen their prayer life; Hindu-oriented seekers who adopted Buddhist practices to cultivate compassion; unaffiliated eclectics who turned (or returned) to Christianity or Judaism because they needed an outlet for devotion; Buddhists who took up yoga or Sufi dancing to integrate the spiritual and the physical. No longer so odd is the makeshift altar in my friend's bedroom. On it is a statue of the Buddha, a crucifix from the island of Crete, a mezuzah, a Zuni fetish, and photos of Ramana Maharshi, the Dalai Lama, and Mother Teresa—all of which have spiritual meaning to my friend. What might appear on the surface to be a breakdown of religious structure might actually be a profound acknowledgment of their common essence. I think of it as a grownup version of the wisdom expressed by three-year-old Sari Zerah. Sari, whose home contains Buddhist art, was walking with her father, Aaron. As they passed a church, she pointed excitedly to a statue of Jesus and exclaimed, "Buddha!" Some might think the child was confused. Some might say she blasphemed. Her father, an interfaith minister, thought she was displaying remarkable spiritual insight.

When you listen openly to new perspectives, your erroneous beliefs and personal biases are exposed. This can be disconcerting, but in the long run it is far more valuable than the false comfort of a flawed or incomplete spirituality. And the opposite can also occur: your core religious values might get reinforced, and some of your tenuous beliefs may solidify into strong convictions because they've held up to scrutiny and comparison.

Your spiritual needs are bound to change at various stages of the voyage. Since it's not likely that one package will satisfy all of your changing needs, the opportunity to shop around would seem to be a blessing—as long as you stay focused, conscious, and informed.

The key, as with so much else, is discernment. Unfortunately, discernment is often condemned as "judgmental" by those who are eager to assert that every spiritual offering has value. Of course they do, but they can't all be of *equal* value, certainly not to everyone at all times, and they are not interchangeable. Since each practice and each doctrine is different from the next, each one is bound to have different effects; we owe it to ourselves to scrutinize carefully what they can and cannot do for us.

> *True religiosity involves an attitude of constant exploration, growth, and self-transcendence.*
> —*Robert Forman*

Smart shoppers are open to the new without being indiscriminate or naïve, and they are selective without being narrow-minded or distrustful. This is not an easy balance to achieve. In my experience, those who manage it well tend to be one of two types. One consists of serious seekers who are looking for something to which they can be dedicated—the equivalent of singles who are ready for a committed relationship and are searching for the right partner. The second group are spiritual veterans who are anchored in a core teaching and wish to fine-tune their repertoire or fill in gaps in their development.

The importance of having an anchor can't be emphasized enough. Even the most confirmed wanderer needs a

bed of his or her own to come home to. A core practice—
something you do regularly enough and long enough to
penetrate beneath the surface—can lend stability to your
explorations. It allows you to keep digging deeper while
at the same time spreading your tentacles widely. And a
bedrock of basic beliefs gives you a framework with
which to interpret and evaluate not only spiritual teachings but also your inner experiences and the events that
cascade around you.

My own experience may be instructive in this regard.
For quite some time I was reluctant to explore beyond the
confines of my spiritual community. The reluctance
sprang from a combination of loyalty, mistrust of my own
judgment, and, perhaps most of all, an arrogant need to
believe that I already had all the answers. Once I broke
through those boundaries I accumulated a variety of practices, which I call upon to meet my varying needs. But
during the heart of the sacred times I set aside, I meditate
exactly the way I always have. I might precede that period
with hatha yoga or breathing exercises or tai chi or an in-
vocation; I might follow it with a chant, another meditative practice, or a prayer. But my core practice has stood
the test of time, and the rest of my bag of tricks is more
effective because of it.

At every moment along the way, the serious seeker has
to decide what his or her chosen path—the *ishta sad-
hana*—must be. Doing that well takes honesty, sagacity,
and self-awareness. As someone once observed, there is
nothing better than a good marriage and nothing worse
than a bad one. Perhaps there is nothing more holy than
single-minded devotion to a spiritual vehicle that works
for you, and nothing more debilitating than sticking with

one that does not. Ramakrishna, whose cautionary remark about spiritual dabbling was quoted earlier, was,
paradoxically, famous for reaching out beyond his native
Hinduism: "How I long to pray with sincere Christians in
their churches and bow and prostrate with devoted Muslims in their mosques! All religions are glorious! Yet if I
display too much freedom, every religious community will
become angry with me. . . Therefore, take me secretly into
the sanctuary of every tradition without exception, and I
will worship ceaselessly with all humanity, day and
night."

TRAVEL TIPS

1. *Don't play the numbers game*. There is no correlation between quantity of practices and spiritual attainment. Amassing techniques and piling up attendance records at seminars in order to keep up with the Joneses is the spiritual equivalent of that obnoxious bumper sticker from the 1980s, "The one who dies with the most toys wins."

2. *Don't judge them by their covers*. The packaging—testimonials, brochures, websites—might not accurately reflect the truth of the teaching. To determine if an offering has value to you, check out its pedigree: How long has it been around? How respectable are those who speak on its behalf? Speak to current practitioners. See if any research or objective reporting has been published. Most of all, pay attention to your gut feelings.

3. *Wear it without alterations*. Respect the teaching by doing it as instructed. If you make arbitrary changes, you might not experience what was intended. And because you've altered it, you won't be able to objectively evaluate the practice.

4. *Give it a fair chance*. In these impatient times, we expect results to come with the speed of aspirin. While you don't want to continue with something that doesn't work, discarding it before it's had time to demonstrate its value can be an even bigger mistake.

5. *Monitor yourself*. Try not to contaminate your judgment with either wishful thinking or fear. You might want spiritual transformation so badly that you convince yourself that the latest teaching is the key to salvation. Or you might be so afraid—of change, exploitation, criticism, etc.—that you run away just when things get cooking.

6. *Look for a foothold*. If you find something that consistently cements your connection to the Divine, why not commit to it for an extended period of time? This can anchor your path, enable you to explore the depths of the teaching, and observe its cumulative effect on your life.

7. *Don't settle for palliatives.* One danger of spiritual independence is adopting only practices that are comfortable and immediately gratifying. The most transformative teachings, however, may be challenging, disruptive, and demanding.

8. *Exotic does not equal better.* There is a tendency to think that the spiritual grass is greener in the courtyard of some other church, temple, or ashram. As we wander far afield, we may, like Dorothy in *The Wizard of Oz*, fail to realize that what we're looking for is closer to home sweet home than we think—on the path we're already on, in the religion in which we were raised, in the book we've already read—if only we can stay awake.

9. Contemplate this stanza from T. S. Eliot's "Little Gidding:"

> *We shall not cease from exploration*
> *And the end of all our exploring*
> *Will be to arrive where we started*
> *And know the place for the first time.*

LOSE YOURSELF

Be melting snow,
Wash yourself of yourself.
—Rumi

Every blade of grass has its angel
that bends over it and whispers, "Grow, grow."
—The Talmud

The dominant American posture is to stand tall and proud, puff up your chest, and declare, "I am Somebody." The dominant spiritual posture is to bow your head, kneel or prostrate, and whisper, "I am nothing." We are urged by some spiritual teachers to yield our will to the authority of a higher power and by others to grab hold of our power and wield it with authority. We are told to stop identifying with our egos—that body-encased, pleasure-seeking, pain-avoiding little self—and to realize the boundless, imperishable Self that is our true essence and knows no "I" or "me." You *are* That, the Upanishads declare. But you are also this. And so we are counseled as well to honor our unique incarnations and work on our minds, our emotions, and our behavior to become the best earthly selves we can be.

IMPROVE YOURSELF

9

ENTERING THE SHADOW, DO NOT TURN AWAY

There is no light without shadow and no psychic wholeness without imperfection. To round itself out, life calls not for perfection but for completeness.

—Carl Jung

A teacher from the East, amused by Westerners' obsession with psychotherapy, shrugged, "If you want to change your personality, do it now. When you're enlightened you won't care."

I chose not to care way ahead of schedule. I thought I could do an end run around my dark side and dash painlessly to the light. Why bother analyzing the small personal self when I was trying to awaken to the big transpersonal Self? Who cares about ego strength when the point is to make the ego disappear? I stopped sorting out the trash in my psyche; instead, I would simply empty it with spiritual practices. My hang-ups, weaknesses, and internal conflicts, my selfish ambitions, and petty desires—all these would be made irrelevant, like wispy clouds that float past the sun without diminishing its light.

Unfortunately, the contents of my shadow did not disappear; they kept washing up on the shores of my life, like cans tossed into the ocean. Spiritual practices did smooth out some rough edges, ameliorating pesky attitudes and behaviors that had been causing me problems—but not always, not all of them, and not forever. My more intransigent patterns withstood the flames of practice like iron bars in a campfire. It took a long time, but eventually I came to the conclusion that the "cushion model"—by which one can presumably accomplish all growth and healing through meditative disciplines—might work for a few fortunate souls, but in most cases our "stuff" is annoyingly stubborn.

> *What are you going to do with your personality, bury it?*
> *You can't bury it, it's like nuclear waste.*
> —*Ram Dass*

I am not the only one to have engaged in "spiritual bypassing," which psychologist John Welwood defines as "the use of spiritual ideas and practices to shore up a shaky sense of self, or to belittle basic needs, feelings, and developmental tasks in the name of enlightenment." I have known countless seekers whose earnest devotion to spiritual development was admirable and whose inner experiences bordered on the spectacular, but whose lives were in disarray. They had neglected aspects of themselves they considered irrelevant to the higher purpose to which God had called them. Some struggled with financial woes and frustrated careers because they had held ordinary ambition in contempt. Some were profoundly conflicted about sex and intimacy. In the name of spiritual freedom, some resisted commitments of any kind. Some were emotional adolescents, as out of touch with their feelings as any alcoholic, because they used spirituality as a tranquilizer. Some were perpetually unhealthy. Like supply-side economists, they assumed that the rising tide of spiritual unfoldment would lift all their boats. It didn't work out that way.

Once you know the peace that surpasses understanding; once you taste divine bliss or sense the presence of God; once you glimpse the pure Self that sits in eternal splendor as a witness to the hubbub of thoughts and feelings; once you say "yes" to the call of your soul, then your spiritual destiny is likely to become your highest priority. The question "What will best serve my spiritual needs?" takes root as the ordering principle of your life. But while lifting your gaze to follow the spiritual banner, you can easily fail to see the potholes. In the name of inner peace, you might avoid anything that makes you aware of urges and traits that you consider unworthy. In the name of transcendence, you might turn away from the challenge of psychological growth. Ironically, when spirituality becomes disconnected from other areas of life, spiritual progress itself can start to drag, for one misaligned wheel can make it hard to stay on course.

The hope that spiritual discipline will make all your problems go away is sometimes supported by evidence. You have the weight of the world on your shoulders, so you pray or meditate or otherwise connect to the Divine, and voila! your burden grows lighter. This often occurs dramatically in the early stages of the journey, when your most pressing concerns begin to dissipate. You assume that the trend will continue.

This wishful thinking is reinforced within many spiritual communities because the members want it to be true, and the teachers, looking down from their lofty perches, say that it is. What lurks in the shadows is either ignored or hurled overboard like flotsam, the better to sail more smoothly toward God.

One teacher, for example, would frequently say things like this: "In the presence of pure bliss, all of your complaints will vanish. Life is a game, not to be taken too seriously." His ardent followers were thrilled to hear this. They did precisely what the master prescribed, and lo and behold, their complaints *did* vanish. Not because their problems went away, but because it was unseemly to complain when your teacher said you'd have nothing to complain about. When one of them admitted that she was chronically depressed and was seeing a therapist, she received this email from another devotee: "You have two choices: You can analyze the depression, find out what caused it, and get 'treated'—then end up more depressed. Or you can eliminate the depression with yogic practice, and not get depressed in the future."

Except that the person he was addressing had been engaged in a repertoire of yogic practices for nine years and, to cover her bases, prayed in church every Sunday. When the beast of depression roared, she would meditate more, pray more, or go on another retreat. When turmoil erupted, she rationalized it as a sign of growth. Eventually, she realized that spiritual practices were not going to turn the blues into bliss. Thanks to psychotherapy and herbal medicine, the depression eventually lifted. In the bargain, her meditative practices had a newfound clarity and silence—a bonus she had not anticipated.

The mind is its own place, and in itself
Can make a Heav'n of Hell, a Hell of Heav'n.
—John Milton

Life does tend to get better when you're on a spiritual path. But progress doesn't always take the shape of a soaring profit line, upward and to the right. Typically, the graph shows choppy ups and downs. When least expected, some buried part of your personality rises up with a roar. This might not matter to monks and nuns. It might be irrelevant in a simple culture with strong communal bonds. But the rest of us have to deal with tendencies we consider ugly or frightening. This is not always pleasant, and it can be hard work. But there are three excellent reasons why shying away from the shadow is not a good idea.

1. *What you resist persists.* By now it sounds like a New Age cliché, but it's nonetheless true: You can run from the unwanted parts of your psyche, but you can't hide. The more you suppress the beasts, the more likely you will be unprepared when they bite you. Left unexamined, they can't be controlled or tamed.

2. *You imprison the good stuff, too.* It's not just harmful, undesirable traits that we hide in the shadows but also some of our gifts: our passions, drives, and unique talents; our exuberance, our creativity, our capacity for ecstasy, and other earthy qualities that complete the human package. We keep some of our treasures buried because their power is awesome, and we fear they'll take control—or because we were taught that our passions will lead us to hell. That they can, when handled

wisely, take us to God is the best-kept secret of the shadow.

3. *It can obstruct spiritual development.* It's not easy to locate inner peace when your mind roils with anxiety. It's not easy to open up to divine love when you hate yourself. It's not easy to taste the rapture of holiness if you're depressed or emotionally blocked. It's not easy to make consistent spiritual progress when frustration, sadness, and worry are your constant companions. And it's not easy to achieve wholeness when you're suppressing vital parts of yourself.

We all want to move toward the light. Unfortunately, we think that means keeping our backs turned to the darkness. We are better served, spiritually, if we look into our shadows with unabashed honesty and usher what we find into the light. Once it is visible we can see it for what it is—not shameful or fearsome, but a part of ourselves we can learn from, dance with, and harness for spiritual growth and human expression.

> *The dark thought, the shame, the malice, meet them*
> *at the door laughing, and invite them in.*
> —*Rumi*

In the early days of psychology, its major proponents were as hostile toward spirituality as Marxists were. When meditative practices burst on the scene a generation ago, some psychologists denounced them as forms of escape, infantile regression, or even "self-induced catatonia." For their part, some spiritual leaders derided psychotherapy as a waste of time, or even as harmful. They assumed that the locomotive of Spirit would pull all other aspects of the self behind it at uniform speed. It seems, however, that every aspect of the self—mind, body, emotional intelligence, social skills, etc.—moves on its own developmental track. But they are also intimately connected, so it is essential to make sure no part of the self lags too far behind, or the whole train will slow down.

Like trees leaning toward the sun, our nature propels us toward greater happiness, peace, love, and wholeness. When we miss the mark, we try to correct our course by diminishing certain traits and cultivating others. Even when we try to stop trying—to relinquish all striving for improvement and accept ourselves as we are—we are *still* trying to grow, only in a different way. And one way we can easily go wrong is to deny, in the name of spirituality, parts of ourselves that need attention. In declaring ourselves to be Spirit, therefore, we have to be wary of refuting our humanness.

TRAVEL TIPS

1. *Explore the terrain.* Through introspection and, if needed, the help of a therapist or spiritual advisor, shine the light of awareness on your unconscious. Examine honestly what's been stuffed away and place it in one of these categories:

Toxic waste. This material is holding you back or is causing harm to you or others. It has to be processed with the aim of eliminating it, bringing it under control, or reshaping it.

Comic relief. Some aspects of the shadow are fixed traits that help shape your uniqueness. They may get in the way at times, but they are relatively harmless. Work toward accepting these traits and, perhaps, observing them with a sense of humor, as if they were characters in a sitcom.

Buried treasure. These untamed aspects of the psyche hold the potential for adventure, passion, joy, and creative expression. Take a walk on the wild side. Explore parts of yourself that have scared you. Expose yourself to experiences that make you feel powerful feelings. But be careful not to go so far that you lose control of the reins. The boundaries that separate enjoyment from over-indulgence and use from abuse differ for each individual. Push the limits of your comfort zone, but make sure you can find your way back.

2. *Don't aim for perfection.* Perfection exists only in the realm of the eternal Self; if you try too hard to perfect the ever-changing individual self, you'll nag yourself to the grave. Can you accept that you are as ridiculous as you are sublime? Can you appreciate the perfection of your imperfection?

3. *Don't lose focus.* While exploring the darkness, don't lose sight of the light. You are not just a collection of "stuff." You are, in your essence, a spark of the Divine. So, as you work on your all-too-human flaws, try to use every problem and every issue as a spiritual practice.

4. *Is it a breakdown or a breakthrough?* History is filled with spiritual heavyweights who psychologists would probably clas-

sify as pathological. We are blessed with the writings of St. Teresa, for instance, because the medieval church made her record her experiences to determine whether she was intoxicated by divine ecstasy or possessed by demons. With examples like that, it is no wonder that some seekers have called their psychological tumult a spiritual breakthrough—only to regret not seeking professional help. Others, however, have dashed to therapists when what they were going through was more of an emergence than an emergency. Some have been incorrectly diagnosed as mentally ill. Get a second opinion, and maybe a third and a fourth.

5. *Choose the right shrink.* To find a spiritually fluent therapist, ask friends and colleagues for referrals. See if your spiritual community includes licensed mental health professionals. Other places to look include yoga studios, New Age bookstores, and professional organizations such as the Association for Transpersonal Psychology.

6. *Medication in moderation.* Can antidepressants be a spiritual boon, or are they a detriment to true awakening? Are they tools for correcting biochemical imbalances, akin to mineral supplements and herbal tonics, or temporary relief with unwanted side effects? These are controversial issues, and you will find convincing proponents of each position. Clearly, it is safer to meditate than to medicate. But, for people with chronic depression, medicine that is properly prescribed and monitored often relieves debilitating symptoms and paves the way for working more effectively on the emotional and spiritual levels.

7. *Don't trivialize spiritual practices.* It's all well and good to use yoga to reduce stress, or to pray for success or chant for healing. But when you use spiritual practices *only* for therapeutic reasons, you fail to harness their full transformational power. They are intended for Self-realization, not just self-improvement.

8. Contemplate this statement from the 20th-century Jewish philosopher Martin Buber: "The face of the holy is not turned away from but toward the profane. It does not want to hover over the profane but to take it up into itself."

10

SECURE ALL BAGGAGE

The past is not dead, it is not even past.
—*William Faulkner*

At a conference on spirituality and healing, two participants had an unexpected reunion. As kids growing up in Boston, Maria and Dennis had been neighbors and sometimes playmates. They had not seen each other since Dennis's family moved away when he was sixteen. Now they were middle-aged colleagues—he a rabbi, she a psychiatrist—with a shared interest in the interface of body and soul. They had arrived at this common ground through widely divergent routes.

Dennis was raised by Jews who were so assimilated that he didn't see the inside of a synagogue until he was invited to a classmate's bar mitzvah. He did not attend a Passover seder until he was twenty and a girlfriend dragged him to one. As a college student, his thirst for knowledge and personal fulfillment drew him to India, where he met his guru. Back home he meditated faithfully, performed Hindu rituals, and switched his major from pre-med to Asian Religions. During another sabbatical in India, his teacher asked him about his own heritage. When Dennis said he didn't know much about Judaism, the guru sent him to the ancient synagogue in Cochin, in the south of India. To his surprise, he was deeply moved by the embrace of the tiny Jewish community. "I felt as though I'd come home," he recalled.

He started to explore his religious roots. At age 26, he had a bar mitzvah. His parents refused to attend. Later, he became ferociously orthodox, organizing his once-un-structured life around the required observances and moving his family to an orthodox community. He would not let his parents visit his home or see their grandchildren unless they conformed to the household rules. Their re-fusal led to estrangement. In his mid-forties, Dennis be-came a rabbi. But certain aspects of his upbringing that had lain dormant—the spirit of open inquiry, the relent-less questioning of authority, the passion for pop culture and social activism—bubbled back to the surface. He loosened the grip of strict legalistic observance and re-joined the broader American landscape. Now he leads in-terfaith programs and features pop music and Kabbalistic teachings at his synagogue.

Maria's family sent their children to Catholic schools and never missed a Mass. Maria was an obedient student and an eager participant in church activities. Then, as a senior in high school, she became pregnant. To her par-ents, and the priest and nuns of their parish, nothing could have been more shameful. She spent the latter part of her pregnancy in what was then called a home for unwed mothers, where she was made to feel like the worst betrayer of Christ since Judas. When her child was snatched away for adoption, she felt so wretched that she knew she would be consigned to hell.

As she matured, Maria's pain and shame metamor-

phosed into indignation. She cursed the Church, rejected its
God of wrath, and repudiated all things religious. But, like
Dennis, she could not entirely escape her past. At times,
warm memories of church came over her: the taste of a
Communion wafer, the scent of incense, the shafts of light
pouring through stained glass windows. She remembered a
sweet feeling she would have during Mass and, sometimes,
in the hush of night, a sense of being embraced by a loving
Presence. She missed it. She missed Christmas too; gift
exchanges and "Happy holidays" had come to seem bland
and empty. But she could not bring herself to enter a
church. Then she discovered the writings of Thomas
Merton, the Desert Fathers, and other Christian mystics.
Her eyes were opened to the possibility of communing with
the Sacred in a different, yet still Christian, way.

Reflecting on their histories together helped Dennis
and Maria realize that the past was exerting a counter-
force on their spiritual progress. They helped each other
do some necessary healing. For Dennis that meant recon-
ciling with his parents and making up for keeping them
and his children apart. For Maria, it meant working
through her anger toward the Church and forgiving those
who had hurt her, for they knew not what they had done.

> *Mindfulness refers to keeping one's consciousness
> alive to the present reality.*
> —*Thich Nhat Hanh*

Most spiritual teachings urge us, in the phrase made
famous by Ram Dass, to "be here now." We are told to
station our attention in the present moment, the only
place where the Eternal can be located. Many take this to
mean we should not reflect on the past or contemplate the

future—a simplistic interpretation that can be hazardous. "Being here now" means being fully awake, mindful, and conscious, not just of one's immediate sensory experience but, ideally, of the infinite Presence that permeates all form and substance. Many of us slip into that awareness from time to time. But the mind intrudes, as is its nature, and it doesn't matter what the content of its meanderings happens to be: contemplating the nature of God may be more spiritual than pondering where to have lunch, but it's still a distraction from the *experience* of God.

It is glorious to stop the mind's incessant buzz and simply *be* in the moment. But straining to do it will actually bar you from the eternal present, just as trying too hard to fall asleep will keep you awake. Also, it would be foolhardy to ignore the practical value of learning from the past and planning for the future. Enlightened masters do those things too, when it is of use to them. The difference is, even in the midst of their ruminations, they remain always and ever Present, witnessing the play of the mind from the box seat of infinite awareness. This is not a mental trick, and it's not a matter of restraining the mind from looking ahead or back in time. It is a state of being.

Wallowing in the past is quite a different matter. Many teachers have warned that obsessing about what has been can be detrimental to spiritual progress. But it's also true that denying your baggage only makes it heavier; it bends your soul like an overloaded backpack bends the spine. The weight of unresolved pain, grief, and regret can make the path seem as insurmountable as Sisyphus's hill. That is one reason why "dying to the past" is a feature of many teachings.

The vast repository of spiritual practices includes

many that break the chain of past conditioning. In addition, various ways to renounce the past—symbolically leaving your family of origin and joining a spiritual family, swapping your wardrobe for the garments of a religious order, replacing a birth name with a spiritual name—have a time-honored value in breaking initiates' ties to their previous, worldly lives. But adopting such affectations because they're cool, or because everyone else is doing it, is spiritual materialism, and it can distract you from practices that are genuinely transformative.

In that context, consider the following anecdote a cautionary tale. When she was a young devotee of Swami Muktananda, Sarah asked for a Sanskrit name like the ones the guru had given to other disciples. He replied, essentially, "See me later." For three years, every time she saw him, she tried to obtain a replacement for the name that she felt no longer defined her. The master was always too busy. Sarah was tormented: "Why does *she* have a spiritual name and not me? What must I do to become worthy of one?" She asked again, this time with greater urgency. Muktananda replied, "Why haven't you expanded?" Once she recovered from that remark, she set about the job of spiritual expansion, content to be called plain old Sarah, which was, after all, a cherished spiritual name.

> *Wash away all my guilt and cleanse me from my sin.*
> —Psalm 51:2–3

Whether rooted in childhood trauma or misguided religious teachings, the past can act like gravity to a spirit that's poised to soar. Children who are abused, neglected, or unloved, for example, often develop an inner core of shame that stays with them throughout their lives. The voices of their hurtful caretakers become internalized, repeating over and over, "You're worthless. You're no good. You're undeserving. You're unlovable." When that message is compounded by religious teachings that emphasize our inherent sinfulness, the shame can be doubly crippling, often leading to either fearful compliance or brazen defiance.

Whereas shame makes you feel that you're some kind of cosmic mistake, guilt simply says that you've *made* a mistake. We feel guilty for things we did or didn't do. Unlike remorse, however, which enables you to take corrective action, guilt is a relentless judge that punishes you for every offense, whether real or imagined. Usually conditioned by parents and other authorities who use criticism as a means of control, the guilt-prone can never quite measure up to their internal standards, and the sense of failure can be spiritually debilitating.

The toxic chemistry of shame and guilt is often compounded by religious fear. In all traditions, the Divine is depicted as having both a wrathful side, which dispenses justice, and a loving side, which bathes the cosmos in mercy and compassion. When the kinder, gentler aspect of divinity is overwhelmed by the voice of judgment, believers tend to tiptoe through life waiting for a thunderbolt to hit or become resigned to spending eternity with all the other sinners.

The word *sin* stems from a Greek term meaning to be off the mark. This can be a useful concept, since we all want to be on target spiritually, and when we swerve off the mark, we all want to *repent* in the original sense of the word: to change or transform the mind. "In classical theology 'sin' is not to be understood as a fault for which someone must be blamed," writes theologian Harvey Cox. "Sin is a bondage from which captives can be liberated." We also need to be liberated from the cosmic paranoia that cripples our spirituality with undeserved shame, guilt, and fear.

For many seekers, the most debilitating hangover from the past is anger. Festering resentment cuts you off from the holiest parts of yourself, making you less capable of love, compassion, reverence, and gratitude. Certain spiritual practices dissolve anger and promote forgiveness and healing. But they don't always reach the long-buried rage that lurks in the corners of consciousness. This may need to be attacked directly with methods such as those in the Travel Tips on pages 110–11.

Bear in mind that ridding your heart of bitterness does not mean you have to reconcile with those who hurt you. Nor do you have to offer them forgiveness. Of course, you stand to gain enormously if you *can* forgive, but you can choose to keep the forgiveness in your heart. The sole beneficiary of releasing your anger is you. Letting it go might require courage and hard work. But the rewards are usually well worth it.

> *Create in me a clean heart, O God; and renew a right spirit within me.*
> —*Psalm 51:10*

In addition to submerged emotions, the repository of the past may also contain religious attitudes and precepts that distort your spiritual vision. It can be helpful, therefore, to glance into the rearview mirror at your early spiritual influences. Contemplate these questions:

SHIFT OUT OF REVERSE

By all means, learn from the past. Expunge every vestige that stands as a spiritual impediment. But don't get stuck there. Think of Lot's wife: looking back at the primitive past, as symbolized by the depravity of Sodom and Gomorrah, can turn your spirit into a pillar of salt.

When you find yourself obsessing about yesteryear, it's time to say enough is enough. Shift into drive by bringing your attention back to the immediate present:

> Focus on your breath: notice the air flowing in and out of your nostrils.

- What was the dominant attitude toward religion in your family?

- How were religious concepts presented to you?

- Were religious threats used to control your behavior?

- Were you encouraged to ask questions, or were you expected to believe what you were told?

- Were you inspired by religious services? Bored? Turned off? Irritated?

- Were religious holidays times of joy or of stress?

- What were you taught about other religions?

- Did religious authorities inspire you? Annoy you? Scare you? Traumatize you?

- Where do you stand with the faith of your heritage now? Do you embrace it? Keep your distance? Harbor bad feelings? Are you indifferent?

Replace the thoughts: mentally sing a hymn, recite a mantra, or repeat a comforting word.

Touch something: put your hand on a nearby object and rest your attention on the tactile feeling.

Name the sensations: inwardly articulate what your senses are taking in, e.g., "I smell the lavender soap," "I hear the wind chimes," etc.

Enjoy the present: "Living well is the best revenge," said the poet George Herbert. It is also the best way to stop obsessing about the past.

Many independent seekers have rejected their heritage entirely. Some turn elsewhere for spiritual transformation but cling to their birth religions for a sense of community, for ethical and moral guidance, or for a historical connection to pass on to their children. Many return to their origins with newfound respect after a long period apart, often bringing with them ideas from other sources. The key, for many, is to secure roots in a tradition without getting stuck in it. But the ultimate measure of any path is the degree to which it connects you with the Divine.

The influence of the past runs deep, no matter how hard we try to escape it. By understanding your spiritual history, learning from it, and, if necessary, healing from it, you can discard what you no longer need and embrace what you cherish. Only then can you truly transcend it.

TRAVEL TIPS

1. *Let it out.* What are the sources of your shame? Who made you feel guilty? Who deceived you, abused you, or crippled your spirit? No matter how long it's been stewing in your system, your rage can be released. Here are some safe ways to do it. They may seem "unspiritual," but what's so spiritual about letting old feelings erode your spirit like acid?

Write letters to everyone who's hurt you. Pour it out on the page; hold nothing back and pay no mind to spelling, grammar, or coherence. No one has to read it; tear it up or burn it when you're done.

With your fists or a child's plastic bat, pound a pillow. Do this in a private space so you can really let go.

Scream and shout. Find a place where you can yell without being heard. Imagine the targets of your anger standing in front of you and let them know how you feel.

2. *Absolve your guilt.* Do you harbor feelings of remorse for actual wrongdoing? Maybe it's time to make amends. What would it take to make things right in your eyes? If you can make a heartfelt, tangible offer of restitution, you might finally be able to forgive yourself and move on.

3. *Fix the leak of regret.* Do you play the same mental tapes over and over again, changing the ending to what you wish had happened? Do a high percentage of your thoughts begin with, "If only I'd have . . ." or "I should have . . ."? You might be wasting energy on regret that could be used to fuel your spiritual journey. Regret assumes that you know things would have been better if you'd done A instead of B. But what you think was an error may have been just what you needed to get to this point in your evolution.

4. *Accentuate the positive.* In searching the past for lessons, we tend to focus on mishaps and mistakes. Don't overlook the treasures you may have buried along the way. What sublime moments can you draw inspiration from? Which spiritual role

models can you learn from? What gifts can you feel grateful for?

5. Contemplate this passage from Eckhart Tolle's *The Power of Now*:

"Nothing ever happened in the past; it happened in the Now.

"Nothing will ever happen in the future; it will happen in the Now.

"What you think of as the past is a memory trace, stored in the mind, of a former Now. When you remember the past, you reactivate a memory trace—and you do so now. The future is an imagined Now, a projection of the mind. When the future comes, it comes in the Now."

11

VEHICLE MAINTENANCE MANDATORY

To get a human body is a rare thing.
Make full use of it. . . .
After getting human, if you don't
reach God, then you have
sold a diamond at the price of spinach.
—*Swami Brahmananda Saraswati*

Melody was a dedicated meditator. For more than 20 years, she began each day with an hour-long Vipassana session. Most years, she would spend two to four weeks in silent retreat, meditating as many as 10 hours a day. Overall, she was satisfied that her consistency had paid spiritual dividends. But she had one area of growing concern: her health. Now in her mid-40s, she had chronic back pain, and at times her hip would get so stiff she felt like an old lady when she stood up from meditation or even from an easy chair. She was also overweight, with high cholesterol. Realizing that her attentiveness to mind and spirit had been matched by neglect of her body,

Melody took up *chi gung* and hired a personal trainer and a nutritionist.

Spiritual traditions present an ambiguous view of human packaging. Some see the body as the enemy of the soul, as in this passage from 2 Corinthians 3:12: "For the flesh lusteth against the Spirit, and the Spirit against the flesh: and these are contrary the one to the other." This split can be so polarized that bodily functions are viewed with disdain, and the passions arising from physical needs are seen as either satanic temptations or desires to be extinguished. Other teachings see the care of the body as important for quality of life in the world, but as unrelated to spiritual growth as polishing a car is to improving its gas mileage.

One common consequence of separating body and soul is that which beset Melody: apathy. Since we are basically just leasing flesh and bones so we can get from class to class on Campus Earth, the thinking goes, our bodies are not worthy of serious consideration. Our job is to awaken to Walt Whitman's revelation: "I am not confined between my hat and boots." Anything that calls too much attention to the space between those two articles merely feeds the illusion that we are defined by our physical form. As a result, a message that was intended to liberate becomes a reason to treat the body with indifference. At its extreme, this can become an excuse for recklessness or indulgence. Since I am more than this physical form, people reason, where's the harm in pouring alcohol into it or feeding it junk or depriving it of rest?

The opposing position holds that care of the body is vital, not only for having a relatively pain-free sojourn on earth, but also for spiritual growth. In this view, the body is the temple of the soul or, as Buddha put it, a "vehicle for awakening." In some traditions, the very purpose of a soul incarnating in human form is to evolve spiritually. Hence the vehicle must be protected, serviced, and maintained in as pure and clean a state as possible.

Sublime vision comes to the pure and simple soul in a clean and chaste body.
—*Ralph Waldo Emerson*

That the physical is a conduit to the non-physical is amply supported by observation and scientific evidence. A number of studies have demonstrated a positive correlation between religious involvement and measures of health and longevity. Add to that the voluminous research on the health consequences of meditation, prayer, and other practices, and it is evident that the well-being of the spirit affects the well-being of the flesh. Why shouldn't it work the other way around as well? Consciousness studies indicate that changes in physiology directly impact the quality and consistency of spiritual experience. This, of course, is a central tenet of yoga philosophy and, to some extent, Taoism, with its links to traditional Chinese medicine.

It is also consistent with the experience of dedicated practitioners. Most spiritual veterans will tell you that the combination of deep silence, heightened alertness, and open heart that is the hallmark of an awakened consciousness is enhanced by strong physiology. If you're in the habit of meditating or praying on a regular basis, notice the difference when you are well-rested, energetic, and disease-free as opposed to exhausted, lethargic, and hurting.

Other variables in the flesh-spirit equation must also

be considered. Some teachings emphasize the need to eliminate the residue of past impressions that get stored in the cells of tissues and nerves—an observation supported by scientific research on the long-term impact of stress and trauma. Esoteric traditions also speak of subtle, powerful forces contained in the body that can be transmuted into spiritual energy. Specific techniques, such as those associated with kundalini yoga, are designed to liberate that power and channel it upward through energy centers (*chakras*) that begin at the base of the spine and culminate in the crown of the head. There are also practices that aim at culturing the ability to apprehend the everyday miracle to which William Blake referred when he wrote "If the doors of perception were cleansed, everything would appear to man as it is, infinite."

> *To darkness are they doomed who worship only the body, and to greater darkness they who worship only the spirit.*
> —Upanishads

Not long ago, I had a visit from a friend whom I hadn't seen in more than 15 years. I remembered him as a fun-loving guy. To my surprise, he'd become a fussbudget. He had to get to bed by 10 P.M. no matter what. He rearranged the guestroom so his head would face east, his prescribed direction for sleep. Every morning he massaged his body with warm oil, making the bathtub as slippery as an ice rink and turning the towels into fire hazards. A strict vegetarian, his meals and snacks were dictated by his Ayurvedic body type, as were the precise times he would eat them. These rules may have been good for his physiology, but they turned him into the houseguest from hell.

It seemed that my friend had become more enfright-
ened than enlightened.

One of the hazards of viewing the body as a temple is
that you can turn the need for maintenance into joy-rob-
bing austerity. Another is to turn body-oriented practices
into ends in themselves, losing sight of their underlying
spiritual intentions. Hatha yoga, for example, a sophisti-
cated system of postures and breathing exercises designed
primarily to foster higher consciousness, can become just
another workout routine. It can even be turned into an
ego trip, as yogis show off how far they can bend and
stretch. Yet another form of excess is to become so self-
protective as to turn into a spiritual hypochondriac. It is
for good reason that many teachings warn against toxins,
sensory overload, and excessive agitation. But the
overzealous turn pollution control into a self-imposed orthodoxy, often becoming as finicky as cats.

There are times, to be sure, when what seems like
squeamishness is actually sound policy. For example, spiritual awakenings are often accompanied by enhanced sensitivity; the senses open up to grandeur that was
previously imperceptible. But they also open up to noises,
odors, and toxins that had escaped detection before. The
world is more sublime, but its irritants are more annoying.
You feel cleaner, but, like a freshly painted wall, you can
be defiled by the smallest speck. Heightened sensitivity
often follows a period of rapid acceleration—after one
adopts a potent new practice, for instance, or attends a
long retreat. Until the spiritual gains become stabilized,
the nervous system can seem like a blackboard on which
the fingernails of civilization constantly scrape. Naturally,
this can make a person extra vigilant.

Nothing wrong with that, unless you become *hyper-*vigilant. One risk is that, like my houseguest, you can alienate other people. But there is an even greater risk: You start to see the world as a threat rather than as a gift and your senses as entry points for pollution rather than delight. Worst of all, you can deprive yourself of experiences that might actually accelerate your spiritual progress.

> *The human body is His sitar. He draws the strings,*
> *and out of it comes the music of the inner universe.*
> —Kabir

To one degree or another, every substance and sense impression that touches our bodies affects our spiritual destinies. The question naturally arises, therefore, "What exactly should we eat, drink, and expose ourselves to?" That's where things get tricky. If you wish, you can find precise instructions on how to regulate each area of your life for spiritual advantage. Unfortunately, the sources won't agree with one another. If anything can be said with confidence, it's that no single set of standards works for everyone. To paraphrase an old cliché, one seeker's ambrosia is another's toxin.

Take the matter of diet. Shortly after I embarked on my own path, I became a vegetarian. I knew I was doing the right thing, not just morally, not just for the sake of my physical health, but also for my spiritual life: I felt lighter and more ethereal; my mind was clearer, quieter, and more attuned. Three years later, I felt weak much of the time. If I went too long without eating, I'd get dizzy and frenetic. Tests revealed that I had low blood sugar, a condition I wasn't helping by eating more cookies than protein. With reluctance and a pinch of guilt, I added fish and poultry to my diet. The change was dramatic. I became more grounded, more stable, more connected.

It was an early lesson in the importance of paying attention to one's individual condition rather than following rules. Along the spiritual byways, I've run into gentle, self-effacing vegans with the light of God in their eyes—and others who were as arrogant and aggressive as professional wrestlers. I've met meat-eaters whose spirits seemed as heavy as lead—and others who ought to be beatified. If there is a bottom line on the food issue, it might be this: the more natural the better. Other than that, listen to your body. If you're ever tempted to settle on a universal rule about food and spirituality, remember this: Hitler was a vegetarian; the Dalai Lama is not.

> *For of the soul the body form doth take:*
> *For soul is form, and doth the body make.*
> —*Edmund Spenser*

Perhaps more important than *what* your body takes in is *how* it is taken in: with what intention, with what awareness, with what attitude. While it makes sense to ask which choice would best serve your spirit, it might also be wise to ask, "What spirit can I bring to this choice?" That goes for everything that can impact the physiology of awakening, whether it's food or music or decor.

Whenever this topic comes up I remember an incident that took place in the 1970s. I was driving from Cape Cod to Boston with a serenely buoyant couple who seemed to float into the car. Not long into the trip, traffic was paralyzed by a thunderstorm. To escape the hazardous conditions, the stressed-out drivers, and the blare of horns, we pulled into a shopping mall. The couple wanted to meditate in the parking lot. I suggested a movie instead. A newly released film was about to begin. My mates had never heard of it, but judging from the title, they thought it might have a religious theme. It was *The Godfather.*

My companions, shaking from sandals to shawls, left after less than an hour. Any more exposure to violence and depravity, they felt, would cause a major spiritual setback. At the time I thought they might be right, but I stayed for the entire film anyway because I was hooked. Only later, when I saw it a second time, did I realize that *The Godfather* has spiritual value beyond its virtuosity. It sets before us the eternal dualities of good and evil, darkness and light, loyalty and betrayal, courage and cowardice, the individual and the social unit—not with the transcendent wisdom of the Bible or Greek mythology, but with far more insight than most popular entertainments. Maybe my friends were wise to leave the theatre. Maybe they knew the limits of what their nervous systems could handle. But I couldn't help wondering if they weren't projecting onto the movie certain preconceptions about what is spiritually okay and what is not.

Seekers often make such blanket judgments: Indian food is spiritual, European food is not; Monet is spiritual, Jackson Pollack is not; Bach is spiritual, rock is not. Well, maybe I'm a heathen, but I find *Hamlet* a more profound spiritual experience than *The Celestine Prophecy*. I love the Book of Psalms, but sometimes Dylan Thomas lifts me higher. An early turning point in my path was being alone in a roomful of Buddhist statuary, transfixed by the serene faces of the Buddhas. But I also find spiritual elevation in

Picasso's distorted faces and the sharp geometry of Mondrian. Billie Holiday's pain, the yowl of a Flamenco singer, or Bob Dylan's rants can sometimes bring me closer to God than a hymn, a raga, or a chant. And the only time I like New Age music is when I'm being massaged.

On the spiritual path, as in art, there is no accounting for taste. But the larger point is this: Whether or not something is spiritually beneficial depends as much on what you bring to it as its own inherent qualities. Not long ago, I was on an early morning flight. Because I could not do my morning meditation at home, I wanted to do it in the plane before breakfast. The environment was not conducive. Passengers maneuvering carry-on bags through the aisle bumped into me. The obnoxious voice of a deejay kept introducing songs better suited for dance clubs. And the man behind me took it upon himself to entertain his seatmates. He spoke loud and laughed louder. I spent my meditation contemplating wise-ass remarks to say to him and mentally composing an angry letter to the airline. Then it dawned on me: Who is more spiritual, a guy who tries to make his companions happy or the curmudgeon in front of him who despoils his own meditation with thoughts of resentment and revenge?

TRAVEL TIPS

1. *Maintain your vehicle.* In determining what is best for you, go beyond the usual health criteria. Do more of what enhances inner peace, alertness, and joy—and less of what agitates, enervates, and depresses. Find ways to be carefree without being careless and vigilant without being a vigilante.

2. *Examine your attitude.* Do you see the body as sacred? Holy? As a distraction? An illusion? A storehouse of "decay, death, conceit, and hypocrisy," as a Buddhist text describes it? A factory of urges and drives that must be overcome? How you perceive your body will, to a large extent, determine how you treat it.

3. *Take delight.* Many teachings call upon seekers to rise above the pleasures of the senses. But while sensory charms can lead to attachment, they can also lead to ecstasy and exultation— and to gratitude to whatever power you wish to thank for creating them.

4. *Breathe deeply.* Whether you call it prana, chi, or life force, the subtle energy that fuels our spiritual vitality is intimately connected with the breath. That is why breath work is central to many spiritual technologies. At the very least, take a full deep breath from time to time. It is a vastly overlooked way to calm the mind and draw vital energy into the cells.

5. *Give it a rest.* Burnout, fatigue, and sleep deprivation foster dullness instead of heightened awareness, agitation instead of peace, irritability instead of love. But being too sedentary can cause similar problems (not to mention other health concerns).

6. *Don't take it for granted.* I've seen believers cancel their health insurance because they were convinced that God, patron saints, or some angelic posse will surely protect them, or that their practices make them immune, or that they can nip illness in the bud with prayer. Faith is a wonderful thing, but it's a good idea to cover your bases. "Pray to God, but keep rowing to shore," advises a Russian proverb.

7. Contemplate these related teachings:

From Isaiah 17:5: "Cursed be the man that trusts in mankind, and makes flesh his strength, and whose heart turns away from the Lord."

From the 19th-century Indian sage Ramakrishna: "He who lives upon havishya-anna [rice and ghee] but does not desire to attain God, for him such food is as bad as beef. . . . He who eats beef but tries to attain God, for him beef is as good as havishya-anna."

12

CAR POOL LANE
FOR LOVERS ONLY

Marriage is half of a religious life.
—*Muhammad*

It is said that Akiva, the 1st-century Jewish scholar, was asked by the wife of a Roman senator what his God had been doing since he created the world. "He makes marriages," replied the rabbi. The interrogator was not impressed. "I own three thousand slaves," she sniffed, "and I can marry any one of them to another of my choosing." To demonstrate her power, she matched 500 male slaves with 500 females. Three days later, she had to quell a bloody riot among the unhappy newlyweds. Humbled, the senator's wife called upon Rabbi Akiva. "You were right," she admitted. "Creation is easy. But maintaining Creation with the help of man and woman—that must take up all of your God's time."

Is romantic love a path to liberation, or is it sugar-coated bondage? Is it a catalyst to spiritual growth, or is it an obstacle? The answer, of course, is, it depends. Riding the spiritual path with the right partner is like having a copilot, navigator, mechanic, and playmate all wrapped into one. On the other hand, being trapped in a bad relationship is like traveling with a nettlesome back-seat driver who tells you to turn in all the wrong places. "It is better to dwell in the wilderness than with a contentious and angry woman," advises the author of Proverbs. If he were on *Oprah*, he'd no doubt say the same of belligerent men.

In all three Abrahamic faiths, the bond between husband and wife is meant to bring both of them closer to God. Both Judaism and Islam teach that males and females were created to complete one another, just as night completes day and day completes night. Christianity also regards wedlock as sacred. In the Catholic sacrament of marriage, for instance, two separate beings are said to become one flesh. In Hinduism and, to a lesser extent, Buddhism, sacred writings define the parameters of marital morality, childrearing, and the like and also provide guidelines for the spiritual advancement of spouses. However, for spiritual purposes, the East clearly favors the hermitage over the hearth. While the ranks of spiritual superstars include a number of householders, most have been celibate monks.

Similarly, while Christianity regards married life as holy, the unencumbered life of a monk or nun has been considered by many Christians the ideal venue for knowing God. Jesus never married, of course, and he didn't exactly tell his disciples to stay home and take care of their families. When asked specifically if it is better not to wed, he says (in Matthew 19:12), "For while some are incapable of marriage[1] because they were born so, or were made so by men, there are others who have themselves renounced marriage for the sake of the kingdom of Heaven. Let those ac-

---

[1] In some translations, the word *eunuch* is used in place of "capable of marriage." It is generally regarded as a synonym for the unmarried.

cept it who can." The unmarried Paul was less equivocal: "To the unmarried and to widows, I say this: It is a good thing if they stay as I am myself; but if they cannot control themselves, they should marry. Better to be married than burn with vain desire" (1 Corinthians 7:8). Later, he hedges: Nothing wrong with getting married, he says, but those who do "will have pain and grief in this bodily life, and my aim is to spare you" (1 Corinthians 7:28).

With these influences, it is little wonder that those who yearn for the glories of spiritual attainment are ambivalent about issues surrounding love and sex.

> *Am I not a man, and is not a man stupid? I'm a man, so I married. Wife, children, house, everything— the full catastrophe.*
> —Nikos Kazantzakis ("Zorba the Greek")

A few years ago, I read that Leonard Cohen, one of my favorite songwriters, had broken up with the actress Rebecca de Mornay and moved to a Zen monastery. My first reaction was one of disappointment: Couldn't he find a way to live in the monastery *with* Rebecca de Mornay?

Like many contemporary seekers, I've always had one foot in a cave and the other in a big house with a beautiful companion and all the conveniences of modern life. My reaction to the Cohen story exemplified that split: the life of a successful, highly respected poet/troubadour with a movie star consort versus that of a monk with no worldly encumbrances, totally devoted to spiritual realization? Hmm. The first choice sounds fantastic, until you consider the hassles, the arguments, the responsibilities, and all the familiar nuisances that detract from the spiritual pursuit. The second choice seems like bliss itself, until you consider waking up alone in an austere bedroom at 4 A.M. to sit with aching knees in a cold meditation hall and then doing kitchen duty with a bunch of guys in brown robes.

Of course, shifting norms have given us a third alternative: We can remain single and still live in the world. At one point, I thought that would be an ideal solution. Without the demands of an ongoing relationship, I could arrange my life to accommodate my spiritual priorities. And without the restrictions of a hermitage I can also have movies, restaurants, music, travel, friends of my own choosing, and all the other earthly joys I'd rather not do without. Even sex! However, while the hybrid life may work for some people, I eventually started to feel as though I were nibbling both a meal and a dessert without being able to dig into either one.

The point of renunciation, after all, is not just to be unencumbered by worldly responsibilities, but to replace them with obligations that are spiritually liberating. Monastic life can entail almost heroic levels of discipline and surrender. Similarly, family life does not just ensure the perpetuation of the species and a stable society, it provides a context for spiritual development. To the extent that the soul is nourished by solitude and freedom, the simplicity of the single life would seem to give it an advantage. To the extent that spiritual progress is aided by the opening of the heart through love and the shrinking of the ego through compromise, compassion, and in-your-face honesty, family life would seem to have an edge.

"The sacrifices of a family are like those of any demanding monastery," writes Jack Kornfield, "offering exactly the same training in renunciation, patience, steadiness, and generosity." I would say "approximately" instead of "exactly." The training is not built into the system. In a monastery, spiritual discipline is constantly reinforced; there is, presumably, expert supervision; there are fewer distractions; and those who falter in their purpose are either put back on course or weeded out. Householders have to be their own abbots and mother superiors, and, unless they adhere to a traditional orthodoxy, they have to create their own spiritual structure.

This is not to say that the only way to move ahead on the path is to take either monastic vows or marital vows. The point is simply this: If you assume that making a commitment to a love partner will slow you down spiritually, think again. And think yet again if you're tempted to walk away from the palace, like Buddha, and find a tree to sit under. The desire to know God or achieve enlightment is not, by itself, a reason to shun intimate relationships. Not if your heart cries out for one. And that cry of the heart is the prime reason that a romantic partnership can be a form of spiritual practice. Especially if there are children in the picture, no other arena offers quite the same opportunity to love naturally and unconditionally. And nothing brings you closer to God than loving naturally and unconditionally.

> *Love challenges us to keep expanding in exactly the places where we imagine we can't possibly open any further.*
> —*John Welwood*

If, as a Zen master reportedly observed, the best monastery for Americans is marriage, what are the rules of the order? The traditional teachings on the subject were, of course, codified in simpler times, before Freud, before the sexual revolution, and before personal fulfillment became a dominant value. Today, a new spirituality of intimacy seems to be taking shape, in which the challenges of coupling and childrearing are not seen as impediments, but as tools for spiritual advancement.

Creating enduring relationships is a tricky business under any conditions. Making them arenas for spiritual growth adds to the challenge, but it also simplifies it. By declaring that the ultimate purpose of your partnership is to move each of you closer to the Divine, you clarify your priorities. The standard by which you measure your choices becomes "What will best serve our spiritual growth?" This by no means eliminates discord. It does, however, shift the bottom line. It also suggests that conflicts can be teaching tools rather than tests of power or battles of will. The question becomes "How can we use this?" not "How can I win?"

Seeing relationship as a spiritual practice compels you to use its demands as teaching tools:

- Disagreements can be opportunities to question your values and biases.

- Conflicts can shed light on behavior that is holding you back spiritually.

- The need to compromise teaches you to be less attached to your desires.

- Having to forgive and accept an imperfect mate can help you forgive and accept others—and yourself.

- Physical intimacy can remind you that the bliss of transcendent union is within reach.

- Emotional shifts can illustrate the impermanence of pleasure and pain, attraction and aversion.

- Being depended upon can be a continuous exercise in compassion and ego detachment.

- Having your flaws exposed can push you toward deeper humility.
- Being loved despite those flaws can open you to gratitude and the love in your own heart.

Love each other, O husband and wife, regarding each other as divine.
—*Hindu scripture*

The spiritual ideal held out for couples in every tradition is to see the beloved as a manifestation of divinity. We are called upon to treat the god or goddess in our midst with devotion, reverence, and selfless love. It goes without saying that the attempt to live up to this lofty goal has to be shared or else it becomes a recipe for inequality. It also has to be held lightly because it is a moving target. In some respects it's easier to see God in a stranger than in the partner who leaves the toilet seat up or is never on time. It's easier to feel compassion for a crime victim on the 10 o'clock news than for the person on the other side of the bed who just criticized you, or nagged you, or let you down. Which is exactly why an intimate relationship can be a rigorous spiritual path.

Because the instinct to become one with another human being is a subset of the mighty force that drives us toward the Holy, relationships can serve as a training ground for the ultimate union. In the context of a strong, spiritual bond, the love that pours effortlessly from lover to beloved is not only its own fulfillment, it is also yeast for the heart. It helps it to expand, so its love can flow beyond its primary target to other people, to other life forms, and, in its fullness, to God.

TRAVEL TIPS

1. If you are in a relationship, ask yourself these questions:
   - On a scale of one to five, how much do you and your partner nourish each other's spiritual lives?
   - With respect to spirituality, what would you like to change about your partner?
   - How can you make your relationship more compatible with your spiritual aspirations?

2. If you are not in a relationship, ask yourself these questions:
   - How much would you like to be in one?
   - How would having a relationship change your spiritual path?
   - With regard to religion and spirituality, what qualities would you like in a mate?

3. *Pave your own way.* Don't feel compelled to choose between two stark alternatives: renunciation or family life. Perhaps your way doesn't fit neatly into either category. Maybe you will walk both paths at different times. In the hills above the holy city of Rishikesh, in northern India, I met a hermit who had lived alone in a cave for more than 30 years, except for three. During those years, he'd been married to a wealthy American. It was interesting, he said, to live with luxuries he'd never dreamed of and to make love with a woman. "But"—and he placed one wrist on top of the other to suggest handcuffs—"it was a prison." Back to the cave he went. Would he do it again? He shrugged as if to say, "One never knows."

4. *Walk a mile in your partner's shoes.* Instead of the consumer-like approach of making sure your needs are being met, the spiritual mindset would be to look for ways to give. Psychiatrist Mark Goulston, my coauthor on *The Six Secrets of a Lasting Relationship,* says that the single most effective solution to any relationship problem is to ask yourself this simple question:

"What is it like for my partner right now?" It is an instanta-neous empathy builder and an excellent ego deflator.

5. *Get help if you need it.* If you need a marriage counselor, you might want to find one whose spiritual outlook is compatible with your own. If you and your partner have serious religious differences or have wandered onto divergent paths, you might look for someone who can relate to both of you, such as an in-terfaith minister or a psychotherapist with experience dealing with spiritual conflicts.

6. Contemplate this statement from the Jesuit theologian and paleontologist Teilhard de Chardin: "Cosmic energy is love, the affinity of being with being. It is a universal property of life, and embraces all forms of organized matter. Thus, the tendency to unite; the attraction of atom to atom, molecule to molecule, or cell to cell."

13

DON'T KEEP SEX
DRIVE IN REVERSE

For the wisest and most elevated among us,
every carnal thought leads to God.
The rest of us must strive toward this goal.
—Rabbi Zalman-Schacter-Shalomi

Bone thin and dour, she wore long, shapeless dresses buttoned to the neck. Her hair was strangled in a steel-tight bun. She carried out her ashram duties with the humorless demeanor of an old-fashioned schoolmarm who can't wait to rap some naughty student on the knuckles. As we watched her in action one day, a friend mused, "I knew her before she was a virgin."

Several years earlier, it seems, she had been quite promiscuous. Now she was celibate and thought everyone else should be, too.

Her turnabout was extreme, but the pattern of flip-flopping from one level of sexual interest to another is hardly uncommon. Some seekers become *more* sexually active once they plant their feet on a spiritual path. Guilt and shame rooted in religious or family history might dissipate; the emotional residue of past sexual traumas might dissolve; the fear of being hurt by love might diminish—

all of which can release old inhibitions and free one's dormant sensuality. Others become *less* sexually active, or active in a different way, or maybe even *non*active. The change might originate as a choice based on ideology or moral doctrines. Some people come to regard sex as a distraction that draws one's attention from higher, more godly pursuits, or as a drain of vital spiritual energy. Sometimes the shift is not deliberate at all, but rather like that of an automatic transmission: The sex drive drops to a lower gear as a direct result of intense spiritual practices. The need for sex becomes less dominant. This can be somewhat disconcerting at first, but it is more than balanced by the fact that sex can also become more fulfilling. Many seekers find it a huge relief to no longer be governed by genital-centered impulses.

After my first long meditation retreat, I felt so liberated by the reduced need for sexual release that I decided to be celibate. I lasted three weeks.

In that rapid reversal I was hardly alone. Apart from the rare exceptions who take—and keep—vows of chastity, most attempts at enforced celibacy don't last very long. The sex drive eventually reasserts itself, but often with a difference. In general, spiritual practitioners are less likely to turn to sex solely as a way to release stress, assert their power, confirm their self-worth, or pacify their loneliness. The direction seems to be: less sexual need, more sexual fun; less sexual compulsion, more sexual fulfillment; less sex for its own sake, more sex as an expression of love.

As for the newly minted virgin in the opening story, some years after I learned about her bawdy past I received a brochure in the mail. She was leading workshops on sacred sex.

> *For some, sex leads to sainthood. For others, it is the road to hell.*
> —Henry Miller

Sex has a split personality in every tradition: It is sacred and sinful, divine and depraved, liberator and oppressor, a vehicle for union with God and the ultimate attachment. In the same Judeo-Christian tradition that we associate with sexual repression, sexuality within marriage is regarded as holy. The same Bible that condemns to death those who commit certain sexual acts also gave us an erotic masterpiece, the Song of Songs. For Christians, sexual pleasure between husband and wife is considered a gift of God. For observant Jews, it is not only encouraged, it is mandated: Men are obliged to satisfy their wives on the Sabbath.

At the same time, strains of religious thought equate sex with sin and regard it as animalistic. To a large extent, we are the heirs of a 4th-century scholar-priest, St. Augustine, whose pithy prayer, "Grant me chastity and self-control, but please not yet," set the standard for sexual flip-flops. In his swing from libertine to celibate, Augustine articulated a theology that left an enduring mark on Western thought. The world was divided into polarities—sacred versus profane, spirit versus flesh—and sex came to be seen as an appetite to be denied except for the purpose of procreation. In trying to understand why it was so hard for him to control his own lust, Augustine came up with an explanation that rings from pulpits to this day:

GIVING IT A REST

On the heels of his divorce, Wayne vowed to be celibate. His stated aim was to secure his children's future, then live the remainder of his life in a monastery. A month later, I asked how he was holding up. He said he was doing just great. He was following the advice that Ramakrishna reportedly gave to men for conquering lustful feelings: "Look upon all women as your own mother. Never look at the face of a woman, but look toward her feet."

Six months later, Wayne said he wasn't doing so well: "I have a foot fetish, and I'm lusting after my mother."

He was joking, of course, but he *was* having a hard time sublimating his libido. A short time later he retracted his

original sin. It is hard for anyone growing up in the West not to be affected by this legacy.

If you think you will get less ambiguity from the Eastern traditions, think again. In the civilizations that gave rise to "The Kama Sutra" and "Counsels of the Simple Girl" (a Taoist-based text thought to be the world's first sex manual), there are elements that are just as conservative as our own Puritanism. For every guru who teaches Tantric sex there are any number who insist that their followers—sometimes even the married ones—maintain celibacy. Some would be right at home discussing sex at the Vatican or the Southern Baptist Convention. A friend of mine found that out the hard way. A deeply religious man, he left his church, sorrowfully, because of its condemnation of homosexuality. His ongoing spiritual search eventually led to India for a lengthy retreat with a

vow. At first he felt like a failure. Then he realized it was foolish to think of himself as a lifelong celibate. He came to view the period of abstinence as a worthwhile learning experience and a welcome respite from an aggressive sex drive.

Many seekers find that a period of voluntary celibacy shifts their perspective on sex and spirituality. Whether it's for a week, a month, or a year, should you choose to take a break, approach it as a sacred adventure, not as an epic battle between spirit and flesh; as a spiritual exercise, not penance or mortification; as an experiment, not self-denial. It can be a chance to learn and to heal, especially if you've suffered sex-related traumas in the past. During this period, treat your body well and take extra time for spiritual practices, especially those that work with physical energy.

teacher he revered. When he arrived he was asked to fill out a registration form. Under "spouse's name," he proudly wrote "Jeffrey." His teacher's reaction marked the end of my friend's discipleship.

> O my dove, in the clefts of the rock, in the secret place of the steep pathway, let me see your form, let me hear your voice; for your voice is sweet, and your form is lovely.
> —Song of Songs 2:14

Sadly, ironically, religious sexual repression has actually worked against authentic spiritual development. Not only are sex-based guilt, shame, ostracism, and fear deterrents to grace, they act like cleavers to sever one part of our being—our body and its passions—from the whole. In another irony, repression has had the unintended consequence of fueling the very sexual excess that has made religious leaders so apoplectic. But while the pursuit of gratification may feel like liberation, it can be seen, in spiritual terms, as just another feverish craving—perhaps the most powerful craving of all—and one that can easily obscure the drive that underlies *all* of our passions: the yearning for transcendence.

For many seekers, reframing the relationship between sex and spirit is a vital step. Rather than see it as a moral or doctrinal issue, it may be more fruitful to ask a pragmatic question: What orientation toward sex will best serve my spiritual development? It might also help to view sexuality as a form of energy that can, like all types of energy, be channeled toward constructive or destructive ends. This perspective enables you to take advantage of practices that convert sexual energy to spiritual use by moving the energy upward, to the centers of love and awakening. It is an orientation that unites flesh and spirit to the benefit of both.

Somewhere between suppression and excess there is a position of sexual balance that is right for every seeker. The basis of the choice can be morality or pragmatism. In the former, you do what is presumed to be right. In the latter, you use the alchemy of consciousness to transmute the raw material of sex into spiritual gold.

TRAVEL TIPS

1. *Contemplate the role of sex in your life.*
   On a scale of one to five, how spiritually rewarding is it?
   Would you say that your sex life and your spiritual life are:
In conflict? Unrelated? Complementary? Mutually nourishing?
   How has your attitude toward sex changed since you've been
on a spiritual path?
   Which words best fit your experience of sex?

Boring	Pleasurable
Compulsive	Release
Ecstatic	Routine
Frustrating	Sacred
Fun	Sad
Guilty	Satisfying
Loving	Tense
Obligatory	Wicked

2. *Sanctify the act.* We tend to think of sex as a means to an
end, namely obtaining the release of orgasm. This not only puts
a lot of pressure on the partners, it diminishes the value of other
aspects of lovemaking. To elevate the experience to a more spiritual level:

- Regard your time together as sacred.
- Create an atmosphere of peace and holiness.
- Consider lovemaking a form of prayer or meditation.
- Take your time.
- Invest touching, kissing, and other forms of intimacy with
  as much value as intercourse.
- Make it okay not to climax every time.

3. *Redirect the energy.* Here is a simple exercise for developing
the ability to control and redistribute sexual energy.[1]

---

[1] Adapted from *Passion Play: Ancient Secrets for a Lifetime of Health and Happiness
Through Sensational Sex*, by Felice Dunas, Ph.D., with Philip Goldberg.

- Seated in a comfortable position, eyes closed, relax completely.

- Imagine your pelvis is filled with warm, golden honey.

- Breathing in, visualize a stream of honey rising from the genital area upward through your spinal column.

- When the honey reaches the crown of your head, hold your breath for 5 seconds.

- As you exhale, imagine the honey flowing down a tube in the center of your body until it returns to the pelvis.

- Repeat the process three times.

- Once you are used to the exercise, gradually increase the number of repetitions until you can comfortably do 81 orbits. Eventually, it can also be done during sexual activity.

4. Contemplate this Zen story. Two monks are walking together. They come upon a stream, where they see an attractive maiden who needs help getting across. One of the monks carries her to the other bank and sets her down. He and his companion continue on in silence.

After a few hours, the other monk can no longer keep quiet. "We took vows never to even look at a woman," he protests, "and you touched one."

"I left her back at the stream," replies the first monk. "You are still carrying her."

14

TAKE THE HIGH ROAD

What does the Lord require of you
but to do justice and to love
kindness, and to walk humbly with your God?
—*Micah 6:8*

They started each day bright and early in the meditation room they had built specially for their company.
When making decisions they aimed for what was best, fi-
nancially and spiritually, for them and their employees.
They were flexible with office hours so everyone could
tend to their souls and their families. The holidays of
every religion were honored with days off for the faithful
and, in some cases, a celebration at the office. They gave
employees time off to do community service. They tithed
a portion of their incomes and gave even more when they
had a windfall—and as stockbrokers in the 1990s, they
had plenty of them. Then they were busted by the Securi-
ties and Exchange Commission for defrauding investors.
"I thought I'd found a loophole in the laws of karma,"
lamented Dave, one the firm's partners, as he pondered his
whopping fine and loss of license.

As a child in the Midwest, Dave's Sunday mornings
were spent at a fire-and-brimstone church, where he heard

that he was a sinner whose only hope of salvation was to embrace Jesus as his savior. At home, the threat of hellfire was used as a disciplinary tool. As a college student, he silenced the memory of strict morality with a cacophony of sex, drugs, and rock 'n' roll, and when he landed on Wall Street, he added money to the party mix. Then he hit the proverbial bottom. After getting sober, he found a spiritual path through the 12-Step Program and a girlfriend who introduced him to yoga to help him detoxify. Soon, he embraced a blend of New Age ideas that held his essential nature to be divine, not depraved. He went from an ideology that calls for obedience to one that centers on inner guidance; from God's wrath to a cosmic hug; from judging himself harshly to accepting himself, even loving himself, as is.

Dave thought his path ran along the High Road, but he had turned onto Narcissist Boulevard by mistake.

During stages of the path when a seeker's focus is on expanding consciousness, getting closer to God, or securing inner peace, the issue of right behavior is often set aside. For those already grounded in a moral code this can work out quite well. But some get self-absorbed and self-important, convincing themselves that their spiritual priorities are so elevated that the ordinary rules of human interaction don't apply to them. Others become as reckless as kids who, liberated from school, dash across the street ignoring traffic signals.

Dave went from feeling inadequate to feeling grandiose; from all rules to no rules. There were clues— angry letters, whispers among employees, preliminary inquiries from the SEC—but he ignored them, like the married man in the old joke who is on his way to have an affair. He cries out, "Lord, if I shouldn't do this, just give me a sign." Suddenly, the bright skies in front of him fill with dark clouds. Thunder roars. Lightning flashes. A tree splits in two. He turns in the other direction, away from the woman, and sees nothing but sunshine and flowers. He calls out once more, "Just give me a sign, any sign."

Dave and his partners believed they were on the cutting edge of spiritual capitalism, and they saw their success as a sign of divine approval. That wasn't their only blind spot. Their runaway ambition had created a kind of arrogance that allowed them to distort spiritual precepts to suit their needs. Were innocent investors hurt by their actions? "It was their karma. They learned a valuable lesson." They twisted the complex concept of karma, exempting themselves from its laws and appointing themselves karmic delivery boys in the bargain.

They had other conceptual tricks as well. Is it not a metaphysical truth that the universe is perfect as is? Is it not true that humans are incapable of comprehending the magnificent precision of the cosmic design? Therefore, who are we to judge what's right and what's wrong? Too bad he wasn't present when the Buddhist teacher was asked by followers about the notion of cosmic perfection. "It is true, you are all perfect," he reportedly said. "Be more perfect."

Sometimes we can be too clever for our own good. Instead of using spiritual principles for moral and ethical guidance, we distort them to justify our ego-driven needs. In doing so, we turn a blind eye to a timeless teaching that runs through all traditions: everything we do—everything we think—reverberates throughout the universe, touching all things and all beings, and somehow, someday, we will reap the rewards of our right actions and suffer the consequences of our wrong actions. Whatever spiritual path you choose, it is likely to include some kind of reap-what-you-sow justice system, whether through a judging deity or the intricate machinations of karma. Like it or not, this puts you in the dubious position of knowing that you are accountable for everything you do.

> To those who believe and do deeds of righteousness hath Allah promised forgiveness and a great reward.
> —Koran (Sura 10, v.19)

In certain theologies, the way to salvation is through good works and righteous behavior. In others, the equation is flipped: Spiritual awakening leads to right action and a higher moral sense. Which is correct? The evidence points to both and neither. Doing good enhances spiritual growth; spiritual growth enhances the ability to do good. However, beware of taking good intentions to extremes. Unless you are truly cut out for the selfless devotion of a Mother Teresa, you might, in the name of service, deny your own worldly needs. In the long run, you can become a martyr instead of a saint.

On the other hand, if you put all your attention on self-improvement and spiritual practice, you can become cavalier about your behavior—to the detriment of the growth you're striving for. The consequences of playing fast and loose with ethical standards are regret, guilt, messy predicaments, the disdain of others, and heavy karmic debt. Keep all your sweets to yourself and you might suffer the spiritual equivalent of insulin shock. If your words and deeds do not reflect the highest ethical ideals, can you truly be said to be living your spirituality?

Most seekers find that sharing one's spiritual bounty comes rather naturally. As you advance on the path, the reverence, peace, and illumined awareness that grows within you pours forth more readily, like water from a tilting pitcher. But to whom much is given, much is expected, and those who have been blessed with a lane on the spiritual highway have been given very much indeed. Wherever there is a choice, therefore, it is incumbent upon any serious seeker to aim for the greatest good: the kindest, most compassionate, least harmful action one can muster without being a sap or a doormat—and without holding yourself to impossible standards, for "The world contains no man so righteous that he can do right always and never do wrong" (Ecclesiastes 7:20).

Taking the High Road may seem to be sacrificial, but in the long run it enhances your personal progress. Every time you do something kind or generous or thoughtful, you leave the confines of your ego and link your awareness to a larger whole, even if that enlargement extends only to the proverbial old lady who needs help crossing the street. Those small deposits of decency yield spiritual returns: greater harmony in your surroundings, the love and respect of others, guilt-free inner peace, and other karmic dividends that arrive at your doorstep in self-addressed envelopes.

> *Be a blazing fire of truth, be a beauteous blossom of love and be a soothing balm of peace.*
> —*Sufi saying*

What are the rules of the High Road? Under some circumstances religious codes can be a flawless guide. At other times, however, they seem ambiguous, bewildering,

STOP FOR EGO CHECK

Humility! The last trap that awaits the ego in search of absolute truth.
—Lawrence Durrell

Feeling proud of your generosity and kindness? Careful! Relaxing on cruise control can be dangerous.

Humility is one of the welcome results of spiritual growth, but it is also a practice of its own. It serves as a form of protection against self-importance, one-upmanship, and other forms of "spiritual materialism." But it has to be gen-

and inapplicable to a world that the sages and prophets could not have imagined. Nevertheless, certain basics are universally accepted.

In ancient Jerusalem, a young wise guy challenged Rabbi Hillel to teach him the Torah in the time that he, the seeker, could remain standing on one foot. "What is hateful to you, do not do to others," said Hillel. "That is the whole of the Torah. The rest is commentary. Now go and learn." At around the same time, another religious leader said, in what became known as the Sermon on the Mount, "Always treat others as you would like them to treat you." Like Hillel, Jesus reduced a complex system of codes and commandments to a single law that is as profound as it is succinct. Muslims know the same principle from the prophet Muhammad: "No one of you is a believer until he desires for his brother that which he desires for himself." In China, the idea was attributed to Confucius as "What you do not want done to yourself, do not

uine. If it is false, strained, or competitive, humility becomes a different kind of ego trip. When you feel proud of how you've conquered pride, or your ego swells because you've become so ego-free, remember: *The object in the mirror may be larger than it appears.*

In the Jewish tradition it is said that we should carry a message in our right pocket that says we are the center of the universe, and in our left pocket one that says we are but specks of dust. The ego, that stealthy trickster, is always trying to nudge your hand into the right-hand pocket. So keep sniffing out what Zen calls "the stink of enlightenment"—that whiff of pride in your own goodness and spiritual achievements.

do to others." The rule we call golden is precious because it encapsulates the eternal verities that govern human decency everywhere: kindness, fairness, honesty, respect for others, and the avoidance of violence, theft, and other infringements on human rights.

If we look into our hearts, we know, in most instances, the right thing to do. It's in the translation from thought to action that things can get tricky, for the ego steps in, like a left foot hitting the brake, with its insatiable desires and its fears, Even the holiest and most pious among us wrestle with that demon. "How to do good I find not," lamented Paul (Romans 7:19) "for the good that I would, I do not, and the evil that I would not, that I do."

We make excuses for taking the selfish way out. We claim ignorance. We blame it on our upbringing. We trump the Golden Rule with clichés about not being codependent or the need to set boundaries. Sometimes we're right to do so. At other times, however, we know we should be more generous. We know we can be kinder. We just don't do it. But the answer to the ego's resistance is often as simple as the advice Miles Davis is said to have given the young John Coltrane. As the saxophonist in Davis's band, Coltrane had started to play the ecstatic, seemingly interminable solos for which he would later become famous. Davis told the prodigy to tame his improvisations. Coltrane said he couldn't help it; the creative rush was so hypnotic that he lost all sense of time. He did not know how to stop. Davis responded, "Just put down the horn, man."

Most of the time we know the rules of the road. We just have to put down our solo-playing ego and harmonize with the rest of the band. As they say in the 12-Step Program, "Fake it till you make it."

TRAVEL TIPS

1. *Metta practice.*[2] This Buddhist technique for cultivating loving-kindness is taught in different ways, but always with the same basic pattern. Seated comfortably, take a few minutes to relax. Then silently recite the following sentences:

May I be free from suffering.
May I be healthy and strong.
May I be peaceful and at ease.
May I be happy.

After a predetermined time, say 5 or 10 minutes, shift the focus to someone whose well-being matters to you. Intone the same phrases for him or her: "May [name of person] be free from suffering," etc.

In the next stage, direct your compassion to someone with whom you're not quite as intimate, but whose relationship you value.

In stage four, shift to someone toward whom you feel neutral—a neighbor, a co-worker, etc.

Next, move on to someone who irritates you, or for whom you have negative feelings. You might feel resistance. Persist anyway.

Finally, send your compassion to all creatures on the planet. Use the same phrases, but begin with, "May all beings . . ."

2. *Use spiritual role models.* In Islam, one of the touchstones for knowing whether your behavior is on target spiritually is that it conforms to how Muhammad would presumably act. Similarly, for many Christians the bottom line is "What would Jesus do?" Think of a revered spiritual figure from the past or present or an exemplary person from your own life (a parent, a friend, a schoolteacher, etc.). When you're in a quandary, imagine that person beside you, guiding you and whispering advice. Make him or her proud.

---

[2]Practices such as these are best learned directly from a qualified teacher.

3. *Don't try to figure it all out.* "The course of action is un-fathomable," says the Bhagavad Gita. It is impossible to know the full range of effects a given action will have as it ripples through time and space. When faced with a complex choice, don't waste time trying to calculate the precise karmic trajectory of all the alternatives. Listen to the angels in your heart.

4. *Don't be hard on yourself.* If your standards are too exacting, you can end up treating yourself unkindly for not being kind enough. You can judge yourself harshly for judging others harshly. Cut yourself some slack. Maybe God's Hall of Fame is like baseball's, filled with superstars who got on base only once in every three attempts.

5. *Cultivate desirable qualities.* Which traits from the following list would it serve you well to develop?

Accepting	Humble
Compassionate	Kind
Empathetic	Loving
Forgiving	Open
Friendly	Patient
Generous	Tolerant
Gentle	Trusting
Helpful	Understanding

Each week, choose one quality you would like to have more of and make an effort to display it in your life. Take a few min-utes each night to reflect on the times you expressed the quality and the times you could have but didn't.

6. *Watch what you think.* Virtually every tradition holds us re-sponsible for our thoughts, not just our actions. They implore us to think kindly, for mental energy reverberates to the ends of the universe and back.

7. Contemplate these words from the 13th-century Christian theologian Meister Eckhart: "People should think less about what they ought to do and more about what they ought to be. Do not imagine that you can ground your salvation upon ac-tions; it must rest on what you *are.*"

15

DO NOT PASS: STAY IN YOUR OWN LANE

I was made merely in the image of God, but not otherwise resembling Him enough to be mistaken for Him by anybody but a very near-sighted person.
—Mark Twain

I was about to give a public lecture with another meditation teacher. Just before we went on stage, I glanced down and noticed that one of my partner's loafers was black and the other was light brown. "Larry, you're wearing two different shoes," I whispered. I expected him to be mortified, as I would have been. Instead, he calmly examined first one shoe and then the other, and said, "They're not so different."

I've always remembered that remark, not just because it was clever and somewhat profound, but because it was genuine. The words rolled playfully off Larry's tongue without a trace of pretense. He was, at that moment at least, beyond embarrassment and inclined to see unity where he might otherwise have seen differences.

The memory stands in sharp contrast to instances in which people *tried* to say something wise or project an air of imperturbable serenity or present themselves as unattached or compassionate—in short, to act the way they assumed an enlightened being would act, when in fact they were troubled, angry, afraid, tense, or otherwise feeling what they believed spiritual aspirants should not feel. Among my compatriots it was common when assaulted by a bit of unpleasantness to say, "Look at the pearly white teeth." This was a reference to the story of a holy man who was said to be in a state of constant celebration of the Divine. A local cynic decides to test the saint by walking him past scenes of horror and depravity. At one point, they come to a dead dog rotting in the street. A putrid odor rises from the decaying carcass. Insects gnaw at the flesh. Gazing at the disgusting sight, the holy man remarks, "What beautiful, pearly white teeth."

The attempt by us ordinary Joes and Janes to see the pearly whites in ugly situations met with mixed results. When done sensibly and prudently, it was a useful training in glass-half-full thinking, a way to accentuate life's hidden blessings and to cultivate gratitude. But some people crossed the line into contrivance. Their efforts didn't just ring hollow, they resounded with the dull clang of artifice. You'd want to shake them and scream, "Get real!"

Most of the time, the manufactured behavior was harmless—annoying at most and sometimes even funny. Occasionally, however, someone's strained attempt to be superspiritual could meet with unfortunate results, like a kid who dons a Superman costume and flies off a roof. I remember someone named Tanya whose boyfriend was having an affair with a married woman. It was a messy, potentially volatile situation, and Tanya tried to be "spiritual" about it. She felt she should rise above petty emotions like jealousy. She thought she should stop judging her boyfriend and offer him compassion and love without conditions. As for her anxiety, fear, and anger, well, they were only transient emotions that she could overcome by intensifying her spiritual practices. Luckily, in the midst of Tanya's trials, a friend was able to convince her that her spiritual lesson was not to passively accept whatever happens to her but to stand up for what is right.

> *Almost all absurdity of conduct arises from the imitation of those whom we cannot resemble.*
> —Samuel Johnson

There are many prescriptions for—and even more assumptions about—the way a spiritual person ought to behave. We are exhorted to be detached, unshakable, and calm under all circumstances; to rise above craving and desire; to extend loving-kindness to all beings; to be nonjudgmental; to always be grateful; to remember God; to love—or at least forgive—our enemies. Okay, sure, piece of cake, no problem. But there *is* a problem. Many of these guidelines are better understood as *descriptive*, rather than prescriptive. They describe those who reach the highest strata of development. Only rare beings exhibit them in full flower, and not because they've altered their mood or practiced certain behavior or worked on their attitude. Precious qualities emanate from them as naturally as purring from a cat.

To expect that by *imitating* the qualities of masters we will acquire what they have is to mistake the goal for the path. It is like donning a number 23 jersey and thinking you can "be like Mike" and soar to the hoop for a slam dunk or like adorning your head with a crown and expecting to be treated like a monarch. The qualities we associate with spiritual realization can't be contrived or willed into being. We can aspire to them and we can try to approximate them, and we might very well derive value from the attempt. But playacting is not only futile, it can be self-defeating—and, in the process, turn off everyone who sees through it. "The strain of attempting to be dispassionate or detached, of trying to make a mood of equanimity in pleasure and pain, only puts unnatural, undue stress on the mind," writes Maharishi Mahesh Yogi. "This kind of practice has helped to bring dullness, artificiality, and tension to life in the name of spiritual growth."

There is another problem with trying to reproduce in ourselves what we think great spiritual beings are like: We don't always have an accurate picture to trace. Some of our images of "being spiritual" are as sanitized as pastoral films of life in the wild that leave out the blood and guts. It is worth remembering that many of the spiritual leaders we revere, from Moses to Gandhi to Martin Luther King, saw what was what, and they told it like it was. For example, many seekers take literally the directive "Judge not, that ye be not judged." We forget that Jesus—the prince of peace, the master of mercy, the turner of the other cheek—made plenty of judgments, driving money-changers from the temple, for example, and dissing the hypocrites and Pharisees. Perhaps a more realistic model to hold before us is of someone who can praise the pearly white teeth and also say, "The dead dog is revolting, it stinks, it spreads disease. Get rid of it!"

In the novel *All We Know of Heaven*, Remy

Rouggeau writes, in the voice of a novice in a monastery: "Real monks do not scratch in odd places when they assemble to hear their abbot speak. Real monks do not belch in the choir. Real monks do not shovel food into their mouths in the refectory. Real monks have manners." The character had fixed ideas of what holy folk would be like, and he was shocked to learn they were human. It reminds me of the time I saw a spiritual teacher comb his hair just before a public presentation. I was shocked. *Holy men aren't supposed to be vain!* Well, we think they're not supposed to get angry either, yet spiritual lore tells of torrents of indignation pouring forth from the same lips that drip the honey of universal love. You would also think that saintly figures who espouse nonviolence would not travel with armed bodyguards. Yet when I saw the Dalai Lama speak to a large audience in India, I found myself seated four feet away from two of the fiercest-looking young men I'd ever seen. The fingers on the triggers of high-powered rifles and the steely eyes scanning the assembly for signs of trouble left no doubt that their presence was more than cosmetic.

We are under the illusion that spiritual adepts don't feel sorrow, grief, and other painful emotions. We think they never display impatience, annoyance, or irritability. It is probably safe to assume that the negative aspects of the human condition rise up in them a whole lot less frequently than they do in us. But the truly salient difference is what's going on inside them. If the descriptions of spiritual attainment are accurate, the holy ones maintain their equanimity even during the ups and downs of existence— not as a mere disposition but as a deep, structural condition of being. They are not likely to agonize over what

I AM, THEREFORE I THINK

Perhaps more insidious than imitating the outer behavior of awakened masters—or those purported to be—is trying to duplicate what you imagine their *inner* state to be.

We are urged to see and feel the way the blessed ones supposedly do: "Be at One with everything," "Feel the presence of God," "Open to your divine essence." But doing those things—really, truly making them happen—is not as simple as following directions to turn at a traffic light.

For one thing, a lot gets lost in translation. Being One

might have been or to wish that anything were different. They are less attached to particular outcomes than the rest of us would be. "Thy will be done" is as natural to them as "At your service" is to a butler. To them, every experience, whether joyful or sorrowful, is holy. And in living those qualities, they are, at all times, authentic.

> *We should learn from gurus, but we should emulate only saints.*
> —*Jeffrey Utter*

What a minute! Why discourage people from trying to live up to a spiritual ideal? Isn't there something to be said for "acting as if?" Didn't you say as much in the previous chapter? Yes. But it makes sense only when the goal is realistic and the effort to achieve it is sensible, honest, and free of strain. It does *not* make sense when it is mere imitation. Imitation may be the sincerest form of flattery, but our spiritual role models don't need our flattery. And if we delude ourselves that imitating them is sufficient, we

with all that is becomes imagining how Oneness might feel; knowing God becomes thinking about God; steadfast awareness of the Divine becomes straining to locate the Divine. Doing such things can help keep you on track. But trying too hard can lead to the mental equivalent of a charley horse. It can also trick you into thinking you've attained something you haven't. Self-realization is not just a memory or an idea or a feeling, it's a state of being. Remembering that you are divine is great, but it is not the same as awakening to your divinity—no more than a romantic reverie is the same as having your beloved in your arms.

might slack off on the harder work that leads to genuine mastery.

There is a more constructive alternative: emulation. To emulate is to strive to equal or excel. Emulating enlightened beings can be analogous to a young artist drawing sketches like Rembrandt's or a student guitarist learning Eric Clapton licks; it might create good habits that evolve into natural artistry. If emulation can help you feel gratitude instead of resentment, forgiveness instead of blame, humility instead of arrogance, it can be a balm for the soul and a tool for spiritual advancement—with this caveat: If it crosses the line into mimicry or self-delusion, it is not only useless but potentially detrimental.

What distinguishes realized souls from the rest of us is not so much their outer behavior, but their state of being. That's what we really want to duplicate. But we can't imitate that the way we mimic gestures and inflections. To suppose that we can replicate the consciousness of enlightened beings by imitating their mannerisms would be like expecting to own the treasures of the Louvre by building a replica of its façade.

> *Men imagine that they communicate their virtue or vice only by overt actions, and do not see that virtue or vice emit a breath at every moment.*
> —*Ralph Waldo Emerson*

We can be only what we are. We can see only what we see, feel only what we feel. No amount of pretense, wishful thinking, or mood-alteration can bring us one step closer to truly seeing God in all things or feeling unconditional love for all beings. In other words, don't put the cart before the horse.

It's wonderful to be as loving as we can, for example, but universal love is more the *result* of spiritual abundance than the way to achieve it. Trying to be nonjudgmental can facilitate understanding, but going too far can destroy discernment and turn you into a moral cipher. Kindness and compassion are noble, but outer displays that go no deeper than "I feel your pain" are no more enlightened than a greeting card. Nor does imitating the spontaneity of legendary Zen masters give you their consciousness; it will probably just brand you as impulsive or weird. Which reminds me of a woman who revered her spiritual teacher. When asked what she admired most about her, she replied, "She is always authentic." And so, she imitated her teacher—until she realized that by doing so she was being *in*authentic.

What about the attempt to be imperturbably serene at all times? Certainly, reaching for that ideal can foster a measure of inner peace. But what if it's merely a false front? Then it can become a recipe for a flat, passionless existence—apathy with a happy face. Or denial, as with people who hide their rage under platitudes like "It's God's will" or "Hate the sin, love the sinner." Trying to wear the clothing of equanimity when it doesn't fit can even be tragic. I knew a terminally ill devotee who was determined to rise above physical pain by the strength of consciousness alone, like the celebrated saints she'd read about. Refusing all help, she suffered needlessly and died thinking she'd fallen short of her ideal.

Emulate the masters. Draw inspiration from saints. But remember that the way to Truth begins with the truth of right now, and where you are is the only place you can start from.

TRAVEL TIPS

1. Describe your idea of a truly spiritual person. What qualities of thought, feeling, and action would such a person have?

2. Choose a spiritual role model, either a living person or a figure from the historical literature. Which of his or her attributes do you most admire? Can you emulate these qualities without straining to be something you're not?

3. When you don't measure up to your ideal of spiritual behavior, do you:

- Punish yourself with guilt?
- Torture yourself with feelings of inadequacy?
- Resolve to do better?
- Accept that you're imperfect and praise yourself for trying?
- Have a good laugh?

4. At appropriate times, ask yourself these questions:

- Am I merely creating a "spiritual" mood or do I really feel this way?
- Am I trying to impress others?
- Am I deluding myself into thinking I'm more advanced than I am?
- Am I suppressing my true thoughts and feelings?
- Am I imitating higher consciousness instead of working to achieve it?

5. Contemplate these words from *I Am That*, by Nisargadatta Maharaj: "Do not pretend that you love others as yourself. Unless you have realized them as one with yourself, you cannot love them... When you know beyond all doubting that the same life flows through all that is and you are that life, you will love all naturally and spontaneously."

EMBRACE
THE WORLD

The world is too much with us; late and soon,
Getting and spending, we lay waste our powers.
—William Wordsworth

If the soul could have known God without the world,
the world would never have been created.
—Meister Eckhart

Few serious seekers escape the thought of escaping. It seems that we would get there—wherever and whatever *there* is— if we could move to a monastery or just live simply and quietly in a cabin in the woods, free of the hassles of cities and earthly affairs. Some spiritual teachings encourage this: We are told that the key to heaven is to ditch our desires and attachments and renounce "the world." But here we are, in the world. There's no escaping what we disparagingly call real life. Even hermits have to eat, drink, and find shelter. How can we be in the world and not of it while we are dealing with jobs, money, and all the attractions and aversions of modern life? We can love it or leave it, but in either case we have to use it, *all* of it, to our spiritual advantage.

ESCAPE
THE WORLD

16

USE ALL AVAILABLE LANES

How awesome is this place! This is none other than the
house of God, and this is the gate of heaven.
—*Genesis 28:17*

As a young man, the great sage Shankara became famous for his debate with the foremost philosopher of
his time. The question the pair debated was: Which way
of life is superior for attaining enlightenment, the householder's or the renunciate's? Legend has it that while
preparing to argue on behalf of the monastic position,
Shankara figured he'd better find out what it was like to
have a family and worldly responsibilities. As a celibate
monk, he did not want to defile his own body. So he pi-
loted his spirit into the remains of a just-departed prince.
The experiment went awry, however. It seems that the
pleasures of the prince's life were so intoxicating, and the
duties so distracting, that Shankara's disciples had to perform special rituals to bring him back. Now more convinced than ever that renunciation was the only way to
go, he argued so persuasively that his opponent conceded
defeat and declared himself Shankara's disciple.

Details like body-hopping aside, the debate resonates

in the lives of seekers to this day. For one thing, many of the precepts that influence our paths were developed by ascetics who renounced worldly involvements, and their way of life invariably influenced their teachings. Buddha, for example, left no doubt of his position: "The household life is a dusty path full of hindrances, while the ascetic life is like the open sky. It is not easy for a man who lives at home to practice the holy life in all its fullness, in all its purity, in all its bright perfection." He held that conviction even though he never rode to work on a crowded bus or filled out an IRS form or had his dinner interrupted by a telephone solicitor.

"We must be saved from immersion in the sea of lies and passions which is called 'the world,'" said the Trappist monk Thomas Merton. The heart cries, "Yes! I'm outta here! Shave my head, if you must, and show me to my darkened cell." It's easy to reason that you would find God sooner, and feel more cosmically conscious in the meantime, if only you could leave behind the meaningless barrage of sound and fury and devote yourself completely to the real business of existence: becoming one with the Ultimate. But then you think about all the things you love about the world. You realize you wouldn't really fit in very well as a monk or a nun. And you do have responsibilities, after all. They may be as trifling in the cosmic scheme of things as a game of dominoes, but on some level they're important. Now what? "Maybe I can change my environment, ditch my job, and dump the people who don't understand my spiritual quest." So you relocate, you feng shui your house, you change careers, you leave your unsupportive lover. But you can't change everything. Even if you came close to creating a spiritual utopia, you would have to take your mind, your emotions, and all the rest of your baggage with you. Merton followed his warning about the sea of lies and passions with: "And we must be saved above all from that abyss of confusion and absurdity which is our own worldly self."

We want to transcend it all, but to transcend means to go beyond, it does not mean to leave behind. Transcendence enlarges and enfolds what is being transcended, but it also includes it. Perhaps, in some mysterious way, we need the realm of change, duality, and materialism to take us beyond it. Maybe that is what Jesus was pointing to with that enigmatic advice about being *in* the world but not *of* it.

> *All we ever do our whole lives is go from one little piece of Holy Ground to the next.*
>
> —*J. D. Salinger*

Henry James advised writers to be the kind of people on whom nothing is wasted. His advice suits spiritual seekers even more than scribes. Our task is to use the alchemy of consciousness to turn the raw material of mundane life into spiritual gold. Ultimately, of course, there is no such thing as mundane. There is only the Divine. The stuff and nonsense of ordinary existence is as much a part of God as a sunset or a birdsong or a temple. But upgrading what we call profane to the level of the holy requires upgrading our awareness.

The Divine is like the wind: It enters through whatever window we open for it and sometimes through cracks we didn't know existed. And yet anyone who claims that it's just as easy to be with God on a jam-packed subway as in the silent woods is either full of grace or full of . . . well, something else. When Elizabeth Barrett Browning saw that "Earth's crammed with heaven / And every common bush afire with God," she was not at a keyboard in a windowless cubicle. When Gerard Manley Hopkins wrote that "The world is charged with the grandeur of God," he was not stuck in traffic on the Long Island Expressway. And when Ramana Maharshi said of the spiritual path, "The obstacle is the mind. It must be overcome, whether at home or in the forest," he couldn't have imagined home as a high-rise apartment with recycled air or the sterile endpoint of an hour-long commute.

The "real world" most of us inhabit is not a quiet village. It is a noisy, denatured world of prefab shapes, sensory bombardment, and strangers. It's tacky, it's crude, it's ugly, it's loud. But it's still God. It's chaotic, but the chaos is still *lila*, the play of the Divine. The windows to the Holy are still there, in the traffic jam and the supermarket and the line at the post office, and one of our jobs is to crack them open every chance we get. If Andy Warhol can find art in soup cans, we can find the Sacred in the laundromat and mini-malls. It's just not as obvious as sniffing the raw earth at springtime or gazing at the stars on a pristine desert night.

How do you turn the stuff of life into sacred currency? The first step is to ask that question. The asking itself shifts the focus of whatever is going on at the moment. Your relationship to outer events becomes part of your spiritual curriculum. So do your sense perceptions, if you strive to see, hear, taste, touch, and smell like an artist, a poet, or a saint. So do your thoughts and feelings, if you use your boredom, your anger, your fear, and all your other reactions to this wacky world as grist for the mill.

This is the essence of what Hindus call karma yoga: using the field of action and reaction to move closer to union with all that is.

> *God resides wherever we let God in.*
> —*Menachem Mendel*

As I was steamrolling toward my deadline for this book, my father took ill and I had to fly cross-country to be with him. I vowed to use whatever awaited me as a spiritual practice. For three nervous, heartbreaking weeks, I tried to remain true to my intention. One thing I learned was how hard that is to do. But because I was conscious of staying conscious, the spiritual lessons kept coming. I could see my demons in action: I felt resentful, I tried to control things I couldn't control, I got impatient, I felt superior to doctors and nurses, I got mad at my frail, faltering father for having smoked all his life, and I did what causes me to suffer more than anything else: wishing that my present reality were different. Because I could see how these tendencies work on me, my ordeal became a useful spiritual practice.

It was a practice in other ways as well. I saw how automatic love is when you get out of its way. I saw how easy it is to serve when you surrender to the heart: My father was thirsty, I got water; his back itched, I scratched it; he ached, I massaged him; he was bored, I read him the sports page; he despaired, I held his hand. At one point, I told myself: This is a taste of pure devotion to the Good; work toward living that way all the time.

I also became more intimately acquainted with certain spiritual verities. Concepts I had accepted as true for so long that they had begun to sound trite now seemed fresh and profound again. In my helplessness, I saw the significance of accepting what you can't change. In the failing bodies in every bed, I saw the harsh truth of impermanence. In my father's passing, I saw that death is in the natural order of things, and even that most certain of certainties is embossed with uncertainty, for we can't know how and when it will come. And I saw that even a lifelong atheist can glimpse the Eternal, for just before he passed my dad said calmly that he was going to heaven, a word he had never used except to mock religion. Perhaps because of all that, I learned that one can find grace even in the sadness of loss. And in spite of all that, I saw yet again how hard it is to let go of a powerful attachment.

> *Living the spiritual life is the attitude you hold in your mind when you are down on your knees scrubbing the steps.*
> —*Evelyn Underhill*

It is one thing to make use of exceptional events like the death of a loved one. What about the ordinary grind? What about the customs of society and the expectations of people who don't share your spiritual values?

For Amanda, a family physician in Connecticut, November was the cruelest month. Her large extended family traveled to Pittsburgh from all parts of the country for Thanksgiving weekend, and the only acceptable excuses were illness and in-laws. Amanda was neither sick nor married. Her spiritual support group was spending the holiday on retreat in the Berkshires. Nothing seemed more appealing than four days of deep silence and the opportunity to give thanks in a meaningful way. Her parents

were kind, decent people, but their religious life consisted
entirely of obligatory Christmas and Easter services. What
Amanda had to look forward to in Pittsburgh was an ear-
splitting, smoke-filled, booze-drenched orgy of food, football, and family baggage. But how could she tell her
parents, who didn't even slow down to say grace before
tearing into their drumsticks, that she preferred to pray,
meditate, and take silent walks with people who ate
turkey-shaped tofu?

In one form or another, Amanda's dilemma is a
common one among seekers who walk a nontraditional
path or take spirituality more seriously than those around
them. They feel like strangers in a strange land. The natives don't get them, and they don't get the natives; they
want to be accepted by others, but they can't quite accept
them; they feel pitied by outsiders, and they pity the outsiders.

As you progress on the path, you may feel alienated
by those who don't share your spiritual outlook. You
might take comfort in knowing that you're in good company. What do you think Buddha's kin thought when he
abandoned his duties and his cushy life? How do you
think the families of Abraham or Moses felt when they led
them out to the desert? As for the most famous family in
Nazareth, check out Mark 3:21: "And his relatives heard
of it, and went out to seize him, for they said, 'He has lost
his mind.'"

For three straight years, Amanda obeyed the call of
her soul and spent Thanksgiving on retreat. She could feel
her parents' hurt hundreds of miles away. She sent them
blessings and tried to dissolve her guilt in the nectar of

MINGLE WITH
THE NATIVES

The story is told of a wild man who would barge into a hermitage and disrupt the residents. He was at his noisiest when the monks were nestled deeply in prayer or contemplation. Periodically, the monks would ask the abbot to do something about it, but years went by and nothing changed. When the abbot was on his deathbed, giving his final instructions, his successor asked, "What should I do about the crazy man who keeps disturbing us?" The abbot replied, "Keep paying him."

People who don't understand your commitment to spirituality can be as irritating as that intruder. They can seem to be edging you off the path, like aggressive drivers who keep

inner peace. In the fourth year, however, she succumbed to pressure from her siblings. As she packed to go to Pittsburgh, she felt as though she were filling her suitcase with resentment. At the last minute, she called a friend to see if it was too late to sign up for the retreat. The friend said, "You're so lucky to have a loving family. What could be a better spiritual practice than to make them an offering of yourself on Thanksgiving?"

Her friend's words were a revelation. "I realized that I was heavily invested in feeling spiritually superior to my family," she said. Her attitude toward the long weekend shifted. Instead of an unwanted obligation, it would be a pilgrimage. She vowed to resist her tendency to judge. When her buttons were pushed, she would take it as a homework assignment from God. By Sunday, having

cutting into your lane. One option is to separate yourself, or at least limit your exposure. In some cases, that might not be a bad idea. But don't be too quick to discard people; associating only with fellow travelers can lead to a kind of spiritual inbreeding that causes tunnel vision and alienation from the larger society. Plus, there is much to be gained from intermingling. Outsiders may disrupt you or tempt you. They may challenge your dogmas. It ain't always easy, but it's worth it if they force you to ground your spirituality in real life.

Can you ignore their silly remarks? Can you express your convictions without sounding preachy or pompous? Can you resist the impulse to convert or convince? Can you use them as teachers? Quite possibly, if you accept them for who they are and treat them with respect, they will eventually do the same for you.

spent the weekend making love offerings, Amanda felt more thankful than at any previous Thanksgiving. The gluttonous frenzy had become as holy as the Last Supper.

> *Wherever your foot may fall, you are still within the Sanctuary for Enlightenment, though it is nothing perceptible.*
> —*Huang Po*

At every moment we face the challenge of turning what seem to be obstacles to the spiritual path into the path itself. How we use the lanes available to us depends on what our individual journey demands at the time. We have to ask how the lunch meeting, the workout at the gym, the surprise phone call, the frazzled mate, the changing of diapers, the paying of bills, and all our other mundane moments can move us forward. How can I turn this into a practice? How can I empty my mind and open my heart to receive this offering? How can I inch closer to Oneness in the midst of all this? What is my lesson plan right now?

It boils down to dancing on a precipice, with total immersion in the world on one side and complete removal on the other. We have to take "real life" seriously and yet live it lightly; to know we're only playacting and yet play each role with impeccable craft. It will all seem absurd and meaningless at times. And it is. But it's also not. It will seem unspiritual. And it is. But it's also not. You'll want to get away from it all. And maybe you should. But maybe you shouldn't. Perhaps the most important step of all is to recognize that "real life" *is* the sacred life.

An architect named Peter had been asked by his spiritual teacher to help renovate her ashram. Peter saw it as a chance for a giant step forward, spiritually. He asked his company for a leave of absence and his wife and children for their blessing. Both were given, reluctantly. As he was about to leave for the airport, his daughter told him tearfully that she would miss him at her graduation. His forlorn son said he would email news of every little league game. Peter felt pangs of remorse. He called his teacher in India. "Being spiritual means being responsible," he was told. "Stay home, do your duty, and think of God."

TRAVEL TIPS

1. *Identify your main spiritual challenge* . Which principles do you most need to work on? Make a list, and then find ways to do that work in the midst of your obligations and your everyday comings and goings.

2. *Play the waiting game.* Waiting is one of the great annoyances of modern life. We usually think of it as wasted time. Can you see it, instead, as an opportunity for spiritual practice? Pray. Chant. Sing a hymn to yourself. Breathe deeply. Be kind to someone who's frustrated. Contemplate the meaning of time. Look around and remind yourself that everything you see is a cell in the body of God.

3. *Reduce speed.* The pace of modern life can overwhelm even the most patient of souls. Slow it down. Stop multitasking. Most of the time, our minds are somewhere other than on what we're actually doing. Can you give it your total, unsullied attention? Can you bring to the act the kind of reverent wonder you might bring to a meadow of wildflowers or a work of art? You are in a holy place, of course, wherever you are.

4. *Be prepared.* Before you begin any activity, whether it's performing surgery or changing a tire, take a moment to get centered, and remind yourself that you are about to make an offering. If you have time for prayer, meditation, or a similar practice, so much the better.

5. Contemplate this passage from Franz Kafka: "You need not leave your room. Remain sitting at your table and listen. You need not even listen, simply wait. You need not even wait, just learn to become quiet, and still, and solitary. The world will freely offer itself to you to be unmasked. It has no choice; it will roll in ecstasy at your feet."

17

CHECK ATTACHMENTS
AT THE GATE

*The soul that is attached to anything, however much
good there may be in it, will not arrive at the liberty of
divine union.*

—*John of the Cross*

Not long ago, I had to find a particular photograph of
my parents. This entailed rummaging through several boxes of old pictures. I thought, "Why not use this as
an exercise in nonattachment and get rid of some things?"
It turned out to be a far more strenuous exercise than I'd
imagined. Some pictures were of such bad quality, or were
so clearly superfluous, that they were easy to discard. A
few of the others were definite keepers; they had unique
value, either esthetically or emotionally. But the rest!
"This is a nice shot of so-and-so or such-and-such. I think
I'll keep it. Then again, do I really need it? Will having it
around serve me in any meaningful way? No, it's just another attachment. Out it goes! On the other hand, it might
be nice to look at it sometimes. Keep it. No, tear it up!"

And so it went, picture after picture, stack after stack.
As I struggled with each decision, two voices argued in my
head. One reiterated everything I've learned about the

value of nonattachment. The other said, "Lighten up. You like the picture, keep it." After a while, I couldn't determine if I was too attached to my old photos or too attached to nonattachment.

Every spiritual teaching advises us to be unattached to the attractions and aversions of the world. In the Western tradition, the best-known expression of this comes from the Sermon on the Mount, where Jesus tells the multitude: "Do not store up for yourselves treasures on earth, where moth and rust destroy, and where thieves break in and steal. But store up for yourselves treasures in heaven, where neither moth nor rust destroys, and where thieves do not break in or steal; for where your treasure is, there your heart will be also" (Matthew 6:19–21). Similarly, the 17th-century Jewish philosopher Baruch Spinoza distinguished between the "love of that which passes away"— riches, fame, etc.—and "the love of a thing eternal and infinite." The former, he said, leads to "disturbances of the mind," whereas the latter "fills the mind wholly with joy." With some minor changes in terminology, either passage could have come from a Buddhist text comparing the impermanence of worldly pleasures with the ceaseless contentment of nirvana.

By using images of rust, moths, and thieves, Jesus seems to be referring to material possessions. The East's best-known statement on the subject has a slightly different focus. In the Bhagavad Gita, Lord Krishna tells the warrior Arjuna not to be attached to "the fruits of action," calling those who *are* attached "pitiful" (or "wretched" or "inferior," depending on the translation). Here the emphasis is on the expectations we cling to in our never-ending quest to maximize happiness and minimize suffering. Instead, Arjuna is told to "take refuge in Brahman," the eternal One, which might be considered the equivalent of the kingdom of heaven. While it takes on different forms, the message of the wise ones is: Don't be attached to anything that is, by its very nature, fleeting; direct your longing to the everlasting Divine.

And it is not just possessions and expectations we're urged to detach from. The list also includes:

- Habits
- Sensory pleasures
- Aversions
- Rituals and routines
- Self-identification (roles, images, and other labels)
- Ideas and concepts
- Biases, assumptions, and opinions
- Conditioned behavior
- People and institutions
- Power and control
- The ego

If the list itself isn't daunting enough, wait till you ponder the question "What does it really mean to be unattached to those things?"

> *Everything together falls apart. Everything rising up collapses. Every meeting ends in parting. Every life ends in death.*
> —Buddha

In the highest sense, nonattachment describes a state of being in which one is so securely stationed in the Infinite that one witnesses, from a place of serene remove, the actions of the body, the sensations of the mind, and the hubbub around us. In this state of abiding bliss, the individual recognizes the Self to be separate from—unattached to—the realm of change and decay in which we function. En route to that ultimate contentment, nonattachment can be invested with a wide range of meanings. It is not only a description of a desirable end-state, it is also one of the means of getting there. Indeed, the entire spiritual path can be seen as a process of freeing oneself from attachment, with each step forward representing a mini-liberation. We can't evolve to higher states unless we let go of the previous state, just as a bud can't blossom into a flower without releasing its budness.

Each act of cutting loose an attachment, no matter how minor, is a declaration. It shouts "I'm moving on. I'm growing. I'm breaking another chain and expanding beyond my previous boundaries." In one way or another, attachments are about I, me, and mine. They serve the needs of the ego. Giving them up says "I'm no longer who I was. I'm more." Above all, it says "I know that the source of fulfillment is within me. It does not depend on anything 'out there.'"

For those who take vows of renunciation, the concept of nonattachment might be clear and simple. But even for them it is far from easy to fulfill. One of the Desert Fathers complained that someone "who has tasted the sweetness of having no personal possessions" can still get bogged down in attachment, as "even the cassock which he wears and the jug of water in his cell are a useless burden, because these things, too, sometimes distract his mind." If distraction was an issue for ancient monks, what are we to do about the constant stimulation of modern life, the things that keep us safe and comfortable, the jobs that provide our food and shelter, and the people who sustain us emotionally and to whom we have responsibilities? What does nonattachment mean in our context?

One thing it *doesn't* mean is indifference.

It is common to see spiritual seekers attempting to practice nonattachment by adopting an attitude of non-concern. I call it the Rhett Butler school of spirituality, after the *Gone With the Wind* character whose most memorable line is "Frankly, my dear, I don't give a damn." But nonattachment is not the same as not caring. It is hard to imagine that Jesus would approve of parents who were cavalier about houses, crops, and other earthly "treasures" that their families needed to survive. It's even harder to imagine Krishna telling his star pupil that he shouldn't care whether he succeeds or fails. After all, he also tells Arjuna to lead the charge against the evil forces assembled on the battlefield. You don't send warriors to battle with a blasé attitude.

Not being attached to the fruits of our actions does not mean we shouldn't care how things turn out. It is, after all, the wish for a particular result that triggers virtually every action in the first place. Nor does it mean that we shouldn't act with vigor and passion. On the contrary, it is a call to put our complete attention on what we're doing in the moment, preferably in the spirit of a holy offering. This not only opens us to the sublime miracle that lives in the present, it makes for more effective action. Since we have power *only* over our actions, fixing on a hoped-for result distracts from the work at hand. It also leaves less room for divine intelligence to fashion something even better than we expect. Freedom lies in doing our best, then getting out of the way.

True nonattachment is rooted in the deep awareness that the things that really count—like grace and love and inner peace—do not depend on outer events. It recognizes that even the most ecstatic experience is destined to fade. As George Carlin quipped, "God can't be perfect; everything he makes dies." Such observations have led many to wallow in existential despair. But not those who know the imperishable reality that underlies all the death and decay, and who understand that it—what some call God—is the very essence of what we are. This is the liberating news that makes nonattachment a fullness rather than an emptiness.

> *We must not wish anything other than what happens from moment to moment, all the while, however, exercising ourselves in goodness.*
> —*St. Catherine of Genoa*

How literal should we take the call to give up our attachments? You wouldn't want to lose your "attachment" to the welfare of your children, for example, or regard your loving connection to your spouse as an "attachment" to be relinquished. You wouldn't want to dismiss as mere "attachments" things that provide comfort and security, or to forgo the joy of art, music, and other uplifting pleasures because you're "attached" to them. Sometimes there is a fine line between being attached to something and loving it, cherishing it, enjoying it, or caring for it in a healthy way. One of the great challenges of the path is to discern the difference. While I was working on this chapter, I asked a spiritual teacher named

Chalanda Ma about that distinction. "Attachment is when you fear losing it," she said. "If I love it fully, I'm completely unattached to it."

This points to an important clue: the emotional charge that accompanies our connection to things. Anxiety, clinging, grasping, desperation—these suggest an imprisoning attachment, as opposed to a commitment born of affection, love, or devotion.

Clearly, we can have nothing and be attached, and we can have everything and be unattached, just as we can love selflessly or love possessively. Long ago, in India, there was a young man named Shukadeva, who had taken the vows of a *sannyasi*, renouncing all worldly pleasures and possessions. Now it was time to find a spiritual teacher. His father, the sage Vyasa, believed that the only person fit for the job was King Janaka. "But Janaka has a family, and wealth, and power," Shukadeva protested. "How can someone who's attached to the things of the world be my guru?" To please his father, however, he packed a small sack with the few things he was permitted to own and set off for the palace.

As he sat before Janaka, servants rushed in to report that a raging fire was coming near. They urged the king to leave. He waved them away. "It is God's will," he said. As the flames drew closer, he remained implacable. Shukadeva grew more and more worried. Soon, he could see the smoke and feel the heat. "This man is no master," he thought. "He's a fool." He grabbed his sack, clutched it to his chest, and started to run. Janaka called out: "Who is more attached, a householder who is content to watch his wealth go up in flames, or a sannyasi who clings to his little bundle of possessions?"

Shukadeva fell to his knees and asked to be Janaka's disciple. But Janaka had another lesson to impart. He gave Shukadeva a military escort and told him to go enjoy the gala celebration that was taking place throughout the kingdom. With one proviso: He was to carry a cup filled with milk. If he were to spill even one drop, a soldier would cut off his head.

The next day the king asked Shukadeva if he'd had a good time. He said he didn't see a thing; all his attention was on the cup of milk. "That is how I live," said Janaka. "I care nothing for all this luxury. My thoughts are centered on God." He added: "Whereas your mind was focused by fear, it is love that concentrates mine."

> The devout seeker is he who mingles in his heart the double currents of love and detachment.
> —Kabir

Whatever path you follow, you will be urged to extinguish the strongest attachment of all: the ego. This can be a slippery road. In some cases, what is meant by ego is really *egotism*, as in self-absorption and self-importance. "There is no room for God in one who is full of himself," said the Baal Shem Tov, the founder of Hasidism in the 18th century. If you take that effort too far, however, you can turn it into a form of self-punishment. I have seen many seekers sit on their talents, crush their ambitions, and settle for lives of purposeful mediocrity, all in the name of keeping their ego in check.

But "ego" in spiritual terms means more than egotism. It is the sense of I-ness that defines us as distinct individuals. It is the mailbox in which everything labeled "me" and "mine" is deposited. Because the ego insists on maintaining the illusion that it is separate from the whole of existence, identifying with it denies us the freedom of Oneness. Hence, spiritual teachings urge us to *destroy* or *annihilate* the ego. But such violent terms should probably be reserved for things that are dangerous and loathsome. It might be more benign to think in terms of *expanding* the ego. "Expand" is also more accurate, since our task is to enlarge our awareness of "I" until it becomes identical with the ego of the universe, or the "I am" of God. This is no more a death than an oak tree is a dead acorn.

That losing our attachment to the self is the ultimate victory of the Self is one of the great paradoxes of the path. By emptying yourself you become full. By becoming nothing you become everything. By giving up you become free.

TRAVEL TIPS

1. *Seek balance.* Strive to skillfully pursue your worthy goals without being attached to the projected outcomes. Strive to delight in the things you have without being attached to keeping them. Strive to be content with life as it is without being attached to it staying the same.

2. *Simplify.* If the aim of the spiritual path is to see the One in the many, the simpler the "many," the easier it is to see the One. My girlfriend, a feng shui consultant, is big on de-cluttering. She has trained me to periodically get rid of things I no longer need. I've found that once I get past certain attachments, there is less to think about, less to protect, less to notice. Not less to enjoy, for the things that remain stand out more, just as in music silence accentuates the notes. Getting rid of stuff frees more than physical space. It makes the mind more spacious.

3. *If it hollers, let it go.* It's not always easy to know if something is an attachment that ought to be discarded—especially when you consider things like relationships, goals, behavior patterns, and opinions. Here are some questions to ask:

- Is it serving me spiritually or holding me back?
- Is it of practical use or just a security blanket?
- Am I clinging, grasping, or coveting?
- How much does the prospect of losing it, or seeing it change, make me fearful?
- Will becoming less attached compromise my responsibility to others?
- Will letting it go make me freer?

4. *Don't be attached to nonattachment.* Some people turn nonattachment into an end in itself, losing sight of its higher spiritual purpose. Don't let it become a source of spiritual pride: "Look how unattached I am!" And don't take self-denial to extremes of asceticism.

5. Contemplate this story about a 19th-century rabbi. Because he was renowned for his wisdom, pilgrims journeyed far and wide to be in his presence. One visitor, astonished to see that the famous teacher lived in a small room with only an old bed, a wooden chair, and a table, asked where his furniture was.

"Where is yours?" replied the rabbi.

The guest was perplexed: "I'm just a visitor here."

"So am I," said the rabbi.

18

STREETCAR NAMED
DESIRE—WATCH
YOUR STEP

Every desire is an unconscious yearning for God.
—*Reverend Michael Beckwith*

Depending on where you look, you might hear two vastly different takes on the subject of desire. In some places you'll be encouraged to go for the things you fancy. You might be offered instructions in how to pray, meditate, or chant to get them. It might even be suggested that getting what you want is a sign of God's favor. In this arena, Janis Joplin's plea "Lord, won't you buy me a Mercedes Benz" is not a satire.

In other places, you'll hear that using religious practices to obtain what you want turns the relationship between desire and the Divine on its head. In this view, desire is the enemy of authentic spiritual development. Not the satisfaction of desires, but the destruction of desire itself is held to be the key to liberation.

Is desire a streetcar to heaven or to hell? It depends on a number of factors, all of which are under the passenger's control. For instance:

1. *Desire for what?* Not all desires are created equal. Wanting to help someone in need is not the same as wanting a Ferrari. The desire to provide for your children is not the same as the desire for revenge.

2. *Level of intensity.* Like the burners on a stove, the flame of desire has different settings, such as hope, wish, want, need, gotta-have, and kill-for.

3. *Level of dependency.* How much do you think your well-being, happiness, peace of mind, or spiritual fulfillment depends upon satisfying specific desires?

> *The Great Way is only difficult for those who have preferences.*
> —Seng Ts'an

For those who take literally the statement above by the third Zen patriarch, none of those distinctions matter. To them, the very existence of desire is the source of human suffering, because even the most cherished desire will, once satisfied, be quickly replaced by another, since all worldly satisfactions are fleeting. In this view, we can gain spiritual freedom only when we stop picking and choosing; stop running toward pleasure and away from pain; stop wishing and dreaming and hoping. Aaaah, what a relief!

I have met a number of seekers who claimed to have stepped off the treadmill of desire. In my experience, 1) the peace they say they have reached is more like relief than the sublime "peace which surpasses understanding" that comes with spiritual awakening, and 2) they haven't really done away with desire, but have simply tamped down its flame or changed its direction. They may have reduced to a simmer the feverish boil of craving, grasping, and striving; they may no longer crave things like wealth, success, and possessions. But the minute you ask them what they *do* want, they have plenty of answers. Their desires might be worthy, even noble, but they are desires nonetheless.

It has often been asked why, if Indian philosophy is so profound, India itself is such a mess. One answer is that the subcontinent's impoverishment is due, in large part, to the misguided notion that worldly aspirations are incompatible with spirituality. On an individual level, trying to eradicate desires from the mind can cause similar problems. It can even drag you further from enlightenment rather than propel you closer to it. Why? Because it is impossible to annihilate desire, and trying to accomplish the impossible leads to frustration and futility, not to God.

The minute you set out to extinguish *all* desires, you entangle yourself in a paradox: you want to not want; you desire to have no desires. So you try to stop the desire to stop desiring, but that too is a desire, and on and on it goes. The only way to stop is to realize that you've defined the problem the wrong way. If any and all desires are obstacles to spiritual liberation, what about the desire for spiritual liberation? And what about the desire for worthy things, like love or friendship or health, or even a nice hot bath or shelter from the rain? If nothing else sparks the mental impulses we call desires, the needs of physical survival surely will. What about the desire to serve others? If the absence of desire is the hallmark of realization, how do we explain the saints who desire to help a suffering humanity?

We should ask nothing and refuse nothing, but leave ourselves in the arms of divine Providence without wasting time in any desire, except to will what God wills of us.

—*St. Francois de Sales*

How did we get the idea that snuffing out desire is the key to spiritual fulfillment? In part from the dualistic strain in all religions that starkly separates the profane from the sacred, and in part from passages in sacred texts like the Bhagavad Gita, in which the enlightened are described as "Free from fear, free from anger, free from the things of desire" and are said to act "without longing, having left behind all desires." In a classic cart/horse confusion, that description of the goal has been taken as how-to advice for getting there. The texts don't say that realization is gained by extinguishing desire; they describe the realized ones as having transcended desire. That point is made clear by this lovely metaphor: "As water continually flows into the ocean but the ocean is never disturbed, so desire flows into the mind of the seer but he is never disturbed." In other words, their state of wholeness and contentment is impregnable, even as desires come and go. The desires that arise in them do not spring from deprivation or discontent. Naturally, they act in order to achieve certain results, but whether or not they succeed affects their inner being no more than winning or losing a game of checkers affects a mature adult.

Ah, but that is a description of those in blissful attunement with the Divine. What about the rest of us with our dripping faucets of desire? Since we *can't* destroy all desires, perhaps we need to question the assumption that worldly wants are incompatible with spiritual progress. Is there really anything inherently unspiritual about enjoying pleasure? Or wanting success? Security? Or even frivolous luxuries? Maybe satisfying desires can be more spiritually productive than pretending they don't exist or stifling them in hopes they'll disappear. In fact, some argue that fulfilling our material desires can actually *aid* progress by freeing up time and providing resources for spiritual pursuits.

Whether fulfilling your desires supports or detracts from your spiritual life depends upon the nature of those desires and the consciousness you bring to their pursuit. In that regard, there is a self-correcting element on the spiritual path: As you move forward, the nature of your desires tends to change. Higher aims replace those driven by greed, power, or immediate gratification. Also, the urgency with which you pursue desires eases as you tap into the source of inner peace. And the anxiety of *not* attaining a particular desire relaxes as you realize that all satisfactions are transitory and their rewards are far less substantial than you once believed.

But old habits die slowly. Until wisdom really sinks in, you can help the process along by consciously nudging your desires in the right direction. You can lower their heat so they do not consume your spiritual aims. You can favor desires that serve your spiritual needs. You can find the appropriate balance between going after what will improve your life and being content with what you have. The trick is to do these things without straining to achieve a state of beyond-desire grace—or deluding yourself into thinking you already have.

Perhaps most important, you can remind yourself

constantly that the ultimate goal of all desires is always at hand. Whether you call it God or Spirit or the Self, the kingdom is, in the words of Muhammad, closer than your jugular vein. The yearning to return to our Source and unite with the Eternal is what propels every desire, just as the commuter's longing to get home is what motivates every turn of the wheel, every push and release of the gas pedal, every surge through an intersection. By turning within, you can have a taste of that ultimate grace with far less effort than you expend chasing after the pleasures of the world. The modern dilemma of not being able to have it all is resolved by having *the* All.

TRAVEL TIPS

1. Questions to consider:

- Do you believe in praying, or using other spiritual practices, to get the things you want? If so, why do you believe it works? If not, why don't you?
- When you get what you want, do you usually: Give thanks? Celebrate? Move on to the next desire? Wonder what the fuss was about?
- When you *don't* get what you desire, do you: Feel let down by God? Think you're undeserving? Think you're being punished or taught a lesson? Conclude that it would not have been good for you anyway?

2. *Check your motivation.* To a large extent, the spiritual implications of desire hinge on your motivation. When you want something badly, ask yourself: Why do I want this? What do I think it will bring me?

3. *Go deeper.* Virtually every concrete desire is rooted in a deeper yearning. In most cases, what you're really after is an inner state: happiness, peace, fulfillment, love, etc. Ask yourself: How will getting what I want make me feel? Then ask yourself if you can achieve that inner state without running after the object of desire. The purpose is not to talk yourself out of anything, but to remember the *real* goal.

4. *Reduce the charge.* See if you can reduce the level of urgency from "I can't do without it" to something closer to "I'd like to have it" or "It would be nice to have it." If you're feeling desperate, consider that it might be a signal that you're off track spiritually: You might be looking outside for what can only be found within, or you may have lost faith that a loving God or a beneficent universe will take care of you.

5. *Practice gratitude.* There is no better way to cool off overheated desires than to be thankful for what you already have. This was never more clear to me than the day I walked along

the cliffs of Big Sur on a magnificent spring day and found myself thinking, "I wish I could afford to live here." Then I realized that I was doing about the most anti-spiritual thing I could
do. I was paving paradise with envy and discontent. As soon as
I returned to the glory of the moment, I saw that having the
means to drive up the coast and see God's handiwork at its
finest made me one of the luckiest people on earth.

6. Contemplate this verse from Rumi:

> *You are quaffing drink from a hundred fountains.*
> *Whenever any of these hundred yields less,*
> *Your pleasure is diminished.*
> *But when the sublime fountain gushes from within*
> *you,*
> *No longer need you steal from the other fountains.*

19

DETOUR:
MEN AND WOMEN
AT WORK

Good for the body is the work of the body,
good for the soul is the work of the soul,
and good for either is the work of the other.
—Henry David Thoreau

Jason had mastered the no-ambition, low-overhead lifestyle. As a bright, congenial 20-something he was able to find work doing this and that, leaving him plenty of time for spiritual practices, pilgrimages, and study. He did not mind sharing shabby apartments, driving a run-down Honda, or living hand-to-mouth—until he turned 30. Fortunately, he'd discovered an aptitude for computers. His skills could have landed him a good-paying job, but he bristled at losing his freedom. Instead, he free-lanced. There were lengthy gaps between gigs, but he earned enough to get his own apartment and upgrade his car, and he used the downtimes as spiritual sabbaticals. Jason was content. God would always provide.

Then Jason started thinking it would be nice to have a family. He understood that doing so responsibly meant reevaluating his approach to work. But he put the thought aside for another day. That day came at a multi-faith prayer vigil following September 11th, where he met Stephanie.

Stephanie's trajectory was the opposite of Jason's. She exploded out of law school like a cannonball, working day and night to build a reputation as a competent, tireless corporate attorney. For her 30th birthday, she bought a house with a view of San Francisco Bay. By the standards of America, she had it all. Then she started to wonder if "all" is all it's cracked up to be. In the parlance of the times, she "had no life." It wasn't just that she was pushing herself too hard, but that the work itself lacked meaning, and her soul had grown barren.

Stephanie began making time to explore her inner life and nourish her spirit. One day a thought bubbled up: She should quit her job and start a consulting firm, to help corporations use some of their resources for the public good. She resisted it. She was on track to become a partner in her firm, and she loved her house and all her goodies. Then the towers fell on 9/11, and she knew that her life had to change. But the financial risk was frightening.

Had Stephanie and Jason met earlier, their attraction would not have gone past their first chat at Starbuck's. Now, each was exactly what the other needed. She helped him see that success was not incompatible with spirituality, that he could promote his business without compromising his values, and that working harder could be a spiritual practice, not a sacrifice. In turn, he helped her see that doing good meant more to her than doing well, that pursuing her dream was a leap of faith worth making, and that living more simply could be a spiritual practice, not a sacrifice.

> *There's no spiritual occupation. Spirit is what we bring to the occupation.*
> —Dan Millman

As the Zen masters tell us, before and after enlightenment we have to chop wood and carry water. But does it matter which wood we chop or how much water we carry? Some teachers say we should just find a relatively stress-free way to make ends meet, stay detached, and conserve our energy for spiritual practice. Others say that the way you earn a living matters a great deal. One of the limbs in Buddha's eightfold path is right livelihood, which has traditionally meant performing work that does no harm to others. The concept has taken on broader interpretations, with many seekers trying to find occupations that aim explicitly at improving the community or the planet. For many, the Hindu concept of doing one's dharma has become the guiding light. Essentially, any activity that enhances one's spiritual development is consistent with dharma; in our work-oriented culture, this is often interpreted as finding your calling, or at least choosing employment that is "right" for you.

But such concepts can have a downside. I've seen people worry themselves sick over what they were "meant to do," or feel ashamed because their jobs don't contribute enough, or resist making a commitment because they haven't yet found their true calling. It's not uncommon for spiritual idealists to feel either that they haven't accomplished enough or that they've sold their souls for a buck.

Serious seekers also tend to have high standards. We want our work to be meaningful, to be challenging but not overtaxing. We want hours that allow for a balanced life; bosses who treat us with respect; congenial colleagues who work toward the common good; an environment free of avarice, dishonesty, and stress. We want not only to love our work but to work at what we love. We want to feel that our work is consistent with our spiritual values and our personal inclinations.

That's a tall order to fill. The idealism—some might say entitlement—that it reflects is surely one reason why the ranks of spiritual independents include so many late bloomers. Those who stake their well-being on career advancement, who don't need time to meditate, worship, or take seminars, or don't care about inner peace or karma have a definite edge.

At the same time, changes in the workplace have made chopping wood and carrying water a lot more agreeable to spiritual seekers. It is more possible than ever, for instance, to create a path of self-employment or to work at home. Flexible hours are easier to arrange. Changing jobs and careers is not only more acceptable, it is actually admired. Nevertheless, even the most skilled, educated, and creative among us can find ourselves earning a living under less-than-ideal circumstances. Then what?

> *The trouble with the rat race is that even if you win you're still a rat.*
> —*Lily Tomlin*

Sometimes the "follow your bliss" model of livelihood doesn't work out. Sometimes it takes a long while to turn your passions into remunerative work, and in the meantime you have to pay your bills by chopping whatever wood is available. Such compromises are often disdained by those who believe the universe always provides exactly what we want, as long as we do our practices and act from the heart. But this can lead to frustration and, in some cases, feelings of inadequacy: "What's wrong with me that God doesn't answer my prayers?" or "I don't have the spiritual power to manifest my dreams. What am I doing wrong?" Maybe you're not doing anything wrong, but the realities of the marketplace are not yet in line with your wishes. At those times, you have to ask not what your work can do for your spirit but what your spirit can do for your work.

The workplace can be a spiritual classroom where we not only learn vital lessons but are tested on a regular basis. Perhaps more than any other area of life, it's where we have to put up or shut up on integrity, honesty, compassion, fairness, and other virtues we claim to hold dear. Do you really believe that we reap what we sow? Are you really unattached to recognition and status? Do you truly value spirituality more than material success? At work you get to walk that talk.

If you doubt that work can have spiritual value, consider the fact that labor has always been a central part of life in monasteries. It is not just the need for food and shelter that keeps monks and nuns toiling when they could be praying or reading scripture. The focused use of the body and mind grounds spiritual energy in the tasks of daily life. And menial work drives home the message that toil is as godly as prayer or meditation, and nothing is beneath us.

The chambers of thy soul expand,
And stretch thy tents abroad;
Clasp Labor in Religion's hand
And aid the work of God.
—*Shaker hymn*

The literal act of chopping wood connects us to the primal forces of nature in a way that turning up the thermostat or driving to Home Depot for chemically treated logs does not. Carrying water from a stream or a well brings us nearer to the elemental source of sustenance than turning a faucet or plopping a jug of Sparkletts into a cooler. Physical acts like chopping and carrying free the mind, whereas the modern versions lock the mind into linear processes such as analyzing spread sheets and negotiating deals. If the routines of the workaday world do not provide ready opportunities to glimpse the transcendent or plug into the sacred rhythms of existence, we have to create our own openings while also living up to our responsibilities.

We also have to be wary of making the arrogant assumption that we, the allegedly enlightened ones, are too sensitive, too "spiritual," to fit in among the philistines. When we wish that we didn't have to be doing what we're doing so we can be more spiritual, we sabotage that very wish by snuffing out the holiness of the moment. Remember Tevya, the milkman in *Fiddler on the Roof,* who longed to be rich enough to spend his days reading scripture? He might have benefited from the story of a scholar who lived that dream. On his way to the synagogue, where he studied and prayed all day, the learned man would pass a simple laborer. He held the dirty, ignorant man in contempt. At the same time, the workman envied the scholar for having time to dwell in the holy books. The two men died at the same time. When they stood before the Heavenly Counsel, the scholar bragged about his piety, his knowledge, and the thousands of hours he devoted to God. The humble workman said he was sorry he had so little time for study and ritual observance, but he had no choice because he had to provide for his family. Guess who was admitted to Paradise.

The wisdom traditions advise us to make our work a sacred offering. We are told to perform every action, no matter how menial, as a form of prayer. We are directed to pour our love of the Divine into the objects we make and the services we render, as if preparing a guestroom for a holy personage. We are instructed to work mindfully and to lend our energy to the job while surrendering our hearts to God. If we do those things, we are promised, the most tedious chores can become holy rituals.

TRAVEL TIPS

1. *Evaluate your attitude.* If your current work is not conducive to your spiritual needs, you can look for a more amenable situation or you can bring a different consciousness to work. Consider the observations of psychiatrist Viktor Frankl, writing about Auschwitz. Some of the inmates, he said, "were able to retreat from their terrible surroundings to a life of inner riches and spiritual freedom." Not to compare your job to a concentration camp, but if it can work in the most horrendous circumstances, don't you owe it to yourself to be open to the possibility?

2. *Find your dharma.* If you're searching for the occupation that would best nurture your spirit, you might begin by identifying the activities that bring you joy, expand your mind, and open your heart. But don't expect magic. Your occupational destiny might become clear only through experience, not in a flash of illumination. You may be cut out for something that as yet has no name. You may have a series of careers. In fact, your true passion may have nothing to do with earning a living.

3. *Turn it into a calling.* Scientific studies have found that people who view their work as a calling have greater job satisfaction and overall happiness. Research also shows that the kind of work one does is less important than the attitude one brings to it. Any occupation can be a calling if it is performed with integrity and a sense of purpose.

4. *Examine your assumptions.* Are you judging your present situation too harshly? Are you holding unrealistic beliefs about what is spiritual and what is not? Remember, the performing arts were once considered unholy. And consider the example of Sri Nisargadatta Maharaj. Regarded by many as one of the premier spiritual figures of the late 20th century, he was a humble Bombay shopkeeper all his life. The shop sold tobacco.

5. *Punch God's time clock.* Consider beginning each workday with a brief ritual. It could be something as inconspicuous as a

moment of silence or a ceremony of your own invention. You might recite a prayer, express the wish that your work may benefit all beings, or declare your work an offering to the Divine.

6. *Find your balance.* If you spend too much time rendering unto Caesar, you'll be too exhausted to meditate or pray even if you find time for it. On the other hand, if you're so busy rendering unto God that you forget to chop wood and carry water, you'll be cold and thirsty.

7. Contemplate this passage from Lewis Richmond's *Work as a Spiritual Practice*: "No matter what frustration and indignities erode our sense of outer dignity on the job, inside we remain vividly alive. No matter how insecure our tenure at work, no one can hand a pink slip to our soul. No one can say to our inner life, 'You're fired!'"

20

FORM ONE LANE THROUGH EYE OF THE NEEDLE

It's a kind of spiritual snobbery that makes people think they can be happy without money.

—*Albert Camus*

In the Brooklyn neighborhood where I grew up, there was a mentally ill young man called Ippish, who would go to the market every morning and buy ten shopping bags for 50 cents. He'd spend the next few hours trying to sell the bags to pedestrians. His price? Five cents each. Not a penny more. I wish I could report that Ippish was so happy buying and selling bags that he was blissfully detached from the fruits of his action. I wish I could say that he saw himself providing a valuable service and that making a profit simply didn't matter. Unfortunately, none of that was true. He approached potential customers with the urgency of a merchant who would not be able to feed his children if he did not sell out his goods. Of course, someone would always make sure he succeeded, and when the last bag was sold, Ippish would heave a huge sigh of relief. No, Ippish was not unattached; he was not beyond desire; he was not at peace in the moment. He just didn't have a clue about money. In that respect, he reminds me of certain spiritual seekers.

In fact, he reminds me of myself. I spent a number of years thinking that anyone who puts a lot of effort into acquiring wealth is lost. I saw around me a culture of acquisitiveness that was rotting the collective soul, and I disavowed it. I pitied people who did things just for money, especially the affluent who thrashed about for more and more, like running backs pumping their legs to gain every last inch of yardage. I knew that money was not the root of *all* evil, and I knew that Paul's actual phrase "The *love* of money is the root of all evil" was an exaggeration. But money was clearly the root of a great many illusions, and it was second only to sex as an object of attachment. I wanted no part of it. I was a Spiritual Guy! My role model was Larry Darrell in Somerset Maugham's *The Razor's Edge*, who spurned wealth and lost the woman he loved because he chose to live a life of subsistence and devote his time to gaining wisdom.

Later, it dawned on me that the *absence* of money might just as easily be called the root of evil. Just look at the things people do when they don't have it—or merely perceive a lack of it. As for corrupting the spirit, I'd been poor by choice and poor *not* by choice, and in neither case was I free or content or unattached. That the issue was more complicated than I'd imagined was made further obvious when I got to know some fellow seekers who, thanks to an inheritance or prudent savings, didn't have to worry about money. They could take workshops, buy books, travel to see spiritual teachers, go on retreats, and also live in comfortable environments. I was jealous as hell. How spiritual is that?

It took a while, but I finally realized, 1) there is nothing inherently spiritual about poverty, 2) life on the financial edge can be as deleterious to spiritual growth as greed, and 3) money may not be a sign of grace, as some would have us believe, but it can certainly be a useful spiritual tool. Come to think of it, Larry Darrell had a modest allowance from a benefactor.

> *We are spiritually ignorant and irresponsible when we make worldly poverty an exemplary virtue. If we are all poor, who will help the poor?*
> —Aaron Zerah

Is money a form of spiritual energy or a form of bondage? How can we reconcile the perennial warnings about the hazards of materialism with the obvious benefits of having some bucks? To the extent that love of money is a detriment, is it okay to *like* it? To the extent that the *lack* of money is a detriment, where does lack end and greed begin?

In an email exchange on this subject, a friend of mine stood by Jesus' assertion that it's easier for a camel to go through the eye of a needle than for a rich man to enter the Kingdom. "A rich man is almost by definition attached to the world of things," she wrote. "He has houses, servants, businesses, and all that wealth to look after. It's hard to see through the delusion of money if you're that caught up in it." But do the rich necessarily have a greater psychic investment in money than the rest of us? We might not have servants and a humungous portfolio to manage, but we have homes and jobs and bills to pay. And when paying them is not easy, *more* of our psychic energy is tied up by thoughts of money. Climbing out of a hole consumes a lot more time and energy than standing on firm ground looking at the view.

This is what I wrote back to my friend: "Who is more distracted by money, a wealthy person who devotes her life to spiritual practice and charitable service, or a hermit who can't stop thinking about where his next bowl of rice is going to come from? Who is more spiritual, the heir to a fortune who thanks God for his blessings and gives to the needy, or the factory worker who hordes what she has and is bitter about not having more? Who is more likely to advance spiritually, the CEO who knows that money can't buy happiness or the social climber in the mail room who thinks it can?"

> *Money is better than poverty, if only for financial reasons.*
> —*Woody Allen*

If we take the camel metaphor at face value, we have to wonder where the cutoff point is. By historical standards, anyone reading this book would be barred from the Kingdom (however you define that term); based on material comfort, even America's working poor are rich beyond the dreams of most people who ever lived. And if being well off were a spiritual liability, why would the Bible be filled with worshipful men and women who constantly beseech God for abundance?

As my grandmother once said, "Rich or poor, it's good to have money." Whether that money is a spiritual asset or a liability depends on why we want it, how we use it, and what meaning we attach to it. When acquiring riches becomes an end in itself; when the drive for wealth becomes obsessive; when getting it requires drastic compromises in ethics or values; when wealth is used to buy power, or ego gratification; when it is spent wastefully and unappreciatively—then all the admonishments about avarice apply. But finding the point of balance between those extremes and a reasonable degree of comfort and security is not always easy.

The task is made all the more confusing because of the contradictory messages we get from spiritual teachers. Some tell us that God wants us all to be rich, and they offer to show us how to harness the universe's abundance. Others tell us to live simply, focus on the spirit, and let the material end of things take care of itself. It is hard to argue with either of those positions when they're presented sensibly, and hard *not* to argue when the former becomes a spiritual version of "Greed is good" and the latter devolves into hardship.

I knew someone who decided to radically simplify his life. To reduce expenses, eliminate attachments, and free up mental space for spiritual pursuits, he moved to a smaller home and gave away his nonessential possessions. This included his car, which he saw as an expensive albatross. His friends admired his purity of intent. But it got kind of complicated in practice. Living autoless in Los Angeles meant riding a bicycle in traffic and spending hours on buses. This drained him of energy, time, and cheer. Spiritually, he had to compromise because he could not get to church easily and had to do his daily meditations at a bus stop instead of in his living room. He ended up losing friends because he became in-

DO YOU BELIEVE
IN MAGIC?

Some teachers say that because God's creativity is infinite and the universe is abundant beyond measure, we deserve all the material wealth we could wish for. They tell of people who received unexpected inheritances, huge gifts out of the blue, or their dream job because they chanted a mantra or recited a prayer or whispered an affirmation to themselves.

Well, maybe miracles can happen. But it would seem wise to give the powers that be something to work with. "God will provide" has to be balanced by "God helps those who help themselves."

The story is told of a struggling farmer who can barely

sufferably self-righteous, and he bugged everyone for rides all the time.

Compare him with an affluent acquaintance who collects art from around the world. On visiting her home, you might think she was the poster girl for opulent self-indulgence. Then you realize that the home itself is relatively modest. She surrounds herself with things of beauty because they are joys forever, not because they have monetary value. She could not care less what her collection is worth. She looks at every piece as Keats might have gazed upon a Grecian urn or Ansel Adams might have framed a view of Yosemite—with reverence. She never stops thanking God for the privilege of having them. I asked her how she would feel if the collection were to perish in a fire. She admitted that she could not be sure how she'd react. "Part of my spiritual work is to love beautiful

feed his family. He seeks the advice of a Kabbalistic rebbe. When the master asks what the farmer does first thing in the morning, he describes a number of religious rituals. "Feed your chickens," says the rebbe. The farmer ponders the message for hidden meaning. I was not properly feeding my soul, he concludes. So he prays even longer and studies even harder. And grows even poorer. Desperate, he returns to the rebbe. "Feed your chickens," he is told. Again, the farmer ponders the three words. Finally, a revelation comes to him. He begins a new ritual: He starts each day by giving feed to his chickens. And from then on, he prospers.

Don't get so caught up in magical thinking that you fail to do the outer work as well as the inner work. As a Muslim might say, "Praise Allah, but tie your camel to the post."

things and try not to crave them or get attached to them. Every time I leave the house I tell myself I might never see it again." Though she is surrounded by priceless objects, it is hard to think of her as materialistic.

Somewhere between disdain and glorification is the proper spiritual attitude toward money and the things it buys. We have to find the posture that best suits our circumstances, our inclinations, and our spiritual needs. Meanwhile, we have to keep our focus within ourselves, on the source of true abundance, and remember the words of the wise, like Lao Tzu: "When you realize there is nothing lacking, the whole world belongs to you."

TRAVEL TIPS

1. What do the following terms mean to you?

Prosperity	Poverty
Abundance	Simplicity
Wealth	Rich in spirit

2. Do you want more money? Why? What do you hope to gain?

3. What are you willing to do to get more money? What are you *not* willing to do?

4. *Invest responsibly*. Like other forms of energy, money can be used for constructive or destructive purposes. Why not make it the root of good and invest in enterprises that are consistent with your spiritual values? There are many businesses that serve the interests of both their investors and the larger community, and mutual funds that invest only in socially responsible companies.

5. *Give some away*. Tithing and charitable giving were not invented solely to provide support for religious institutions and to help the poor, but also to benefit the giver. Even if you think you can't afford it—perhaps *especially* if you think you can't afford it—giving away some of what you have is a subtle way of loosening the grip of attachment and opening the heart to wider connections. Finding out that you can be generous even when you feel needy is a revelation that can carry over to other ways of giving. It also sends a message to the universe that you have faith in its abundance. If we do reap what we sow, then your giving should come back to you with interest, if not in cash, then certainly in love, gratitude, inner peace, and other rewards.

6. *Be thankful*. You may think you don't have enough, and you may have excellent reasons for wanting more. But it's also true that if you were able to buy this book, and if you have the time to read it, a comfortable chair to read it in, an electric light to read it by, and food, heat, running water, and other civilized amenities, you are probably the envy of much of the world. And

if you are affluent by American standards, you are a maharaja by global standards. Are you grateful for your riches?

7. Contemplate the deepest meaning of these related statements of Jesus. First, from the Sermon on the Mount: "Behold the fowls of the air: For they sow not, neither do they reap, nor gather into barns; yet your heavenly Father feedeth them. Are ye not much better than they?" (Matthew 6:25–26). And from the scene with the woman at the well (John 4:13–14): "Everyone who drinks of this water will thirst again; but whoever drinks of the water that I will give him shall never thirst; but the water that I will give him will become in him a well of water springing up to eternal life."

21

LEAVE AREA BETTER
THAN YOU FOUND IT

Faith by itself, if it has no works, is dead.
—James 2:17

As a political activist in the 1960s, I believed the Marxist maxim that religion was the opium of the people. Then I became a spiritual activist who believed that *politics* was the opium of the people. I spent several years blissfully detached from world events. Vietnam, which had once drawn me to the barricades, became as removed as the Crimean War. I observed Watergate as if it were a Shakespearean tragedy and other major events as if they were sketches on *Saturday Night Live*.

During that time, I had an exchange of letters with a radical sociologist who had been my mentor in college. In describing my new outlook, I told him that a strategy for social change is like a game plan in football or the choreography for a ballet: It can be as brilliant as anything Vince Lombardi or Agnes de Mille might devise, but if the players or dancers—i.e., individual human beings—are selfish, tense, unhappy, and cloudy-minded, it's not worth the paper it's written on.

In his response, my former professor wrote, among

other things, "If I were a power in the Pentagon, a war-maker in the Nixon cabinet, a racist demagogue in the south, I would say to all of the good and decent youth in America: Stop demonstrating and go find inner harmony! Go to churches and synagogues and mystic shrines and meditate!" In response to my assertion that I was not copping out, he wrote, "Come on, be happy with your inner peace, but don't sell me such a shallow denial."

I wrote back that I was not indifferent to the suffering of humanity. I was becoming a meditation teacher to help individuals find inner peace and higher awareness. If enough people achieved that, I contended, violence, hatred, and oppression would disappear, like the nighttime fears of children when the light is turned on.

He wrote back, "I hope that while you are in India, America finds its pathway and that you return to a wonderful country. But if we have further declined, your meditation will have, in some very small way, made a contribution to that demise, because it will have removed from the political struggle some of our best youth, such as you."

Years later, when I reread his letters, I realized that he had been right about many things. And so had I.

> *The readiness to really live in relationship with God requires reaching back to help others.*
> —*Black Elk*

Many seekers believe they are doing enough to heal the planet by becoming as loving and compassionate as they can be. Some pray or meditate for the welfare of all beings. Some join in communal prayer aimed at alleviating collective pain. Others believe in direct social en-

gagement. Those trying to apply spiritual principles to social ills include everyone from volunteers in hospitals and
shelters, to lobbyists who promote legislative agendas, to
firebrands who rally on behalf of every conceivable position on the socio-religious spectrum. If they agree on anything, it is this: We owe something to the world.

To a large extent, the will to do good is a natural out-
growth of spiritual development. The more connected we
are to the infinite generosity of the universe, the more generous we feel. The more content we are, the more "How
can I help?" replaces "What do I want?" The more expanded our sense of "I" and "we," the more we feel the
concern that flows from kinship with other beings. In the
biblical image of Jacob's ladder, angels not only ascend
but also descend. The message seems to be: It is not
enough for a soul to rise to heavenly heights; the awakened spirit must return to earth, presumably to help out.
Our most revered spiritual figures exemplify this: Rather
than bask in bliss under a tree or atop a mountain, they
accepted the mission of healing the wounded and waking
up the sleepwalking masses. That's what happens when
the divine will flows through one's mind like blood
through veins.

Spiritual teachings don't take any chances, however.
To counter the temptation of wallowing in inner peace,
they make it a virtual commandment to contribute to the
greater good. Christians call it charity. Hindus call it *seva,*
or service. One of the five pillars of Islam is *zakat,* which
obliges Muslims to tithe to the poor. Jews call it *tzed-
dakah,* acts of righteousness, and are pressed into service
by the concept of *tikkun olam,* which means to repair the
world. Even Buddhism, with its emphasis on renunciation

and detachment, calls upon followers to dedicate their practices to all beings and holds as its highest ideal the *bodhisattva*, who gives up his or her final liberation to help end the suffering of humankind.

One reason for the universal call to service is that human beings need each other. The more we extend our circle of concern beyond our own little tribes, the better off we all are. The other reason that charity and service are emphasized in every spiritual tradition is that they bring the giver closer to the Divine. By serving selflessly, we serve ourselves. When we think only about our own needs and wants, our minds focus on what we don't yet have, on problems to be solved and desires to be satisfied. By contrast, thinking about others transports our awareness beyond the ego, linking us to a larger whole. If the links keep expanding, we become linked to the All.

A long-time spiritual practitioner I know earned her living by selling real estate in the tonier neighborhoods of Los Angeles. Then, in her late 40s, this petite, almost frail-looking woman became a social worker. Now, she gets paid far less money to spend her days in the seamiest sections of the inner city. She goes to rehab centers to meet with junkies who abandoned their kids. She visits sordid jails to talk to prisoners serving time for heinous acts. She walks on streets where people are assaulted on a regular basis. And in her hole-in-the-wall office she battles bureaucrats and red tape. Why did she switch careers? "I see it as an opportunity to express my spirituality," she says. "It's a channel for my heart to flow in. Every day, I have to find the good in people who have done bad things, and give hope to people who have none. Yet I walk away feeling like *I* got something out of it."

Selfless service is both humbling and elevating. It can even be transcendent. Not long ago, I was asked what my most powerful spiritual experience has been. I thought of times when I was at one with the universe. I remembered moments of ecstatic bliss. But I found myself giving a very different answer. My most profound spiritual experience, I said, came late one night in a smoke-filled house in New Jersey, when my father took ill and lost control of his bowels. As I waited for the paramedics, I had to wipe his legs clean of feces and remove his soiled underpants. At three in the morning, I returned from the hospital and scrubbed the floor. As I finally got ready for bed, instead of the exhaustion I should have been feeling, I felt a surge of something so apparently incongruous that it took a while to identify it. It was gratitude. I then realized that I hadn't given a thought to myself in more than five hours. It had been the purest, most uncomplicated act of giving I'd ever experienced, and from it flowed a profound grace.

Maybe it would have been different if I'd had to do such things on a daily basis. Maybe for nurses, parents, and other caretakers, such moments are too commonplace to warrant attention. But for me it was a revelation, as such experiences tend to be for those who suddenly shift from self-absorption to self-surrender.

> *The poor, the orphan, the captive—feed them for the love of God alone, desiring no reward, nor even thanks.*
> *—Islamic saying*

The planet needs the help of its spiritually conscious inhabitants. Only those with compassionate hearts and global awareness can counteract the greed and tribalism

SPIRITUAL CORRECTNESS

Certain spiritual concepts are often used to justify detachment from social issues: Everything happens for a reason;
God works in mysterious ways; It's just karma; It must be
God's will; Who are we to judge? Similarly, when conflict
arises, the gentle spiritual virtues—tolerance, forgiveness,
understanding, compassion—seem to be on the side of the
angels, as compared to those demanding force. Then a
horror like 9/11 comes along, and our spiritual ideals are
forced to descend from abstract philosophy to the proving
ground of real life. No wonder that the aftermath saw religious leaders struggling with their long-held assumptions and

that repeatedly place humanity in a precarious position.
We need people who *live* spiritual values not just talk
about them, who *apply* spiritual principles not just hide
behind them or use them as a rallying cry for fanaticism.
We need people who can illuminate in word and deed the
unity behind our vast diversity, to counteract those who
would exploit that diversity and divide us further.

Certainly, not every seeker is also a warrior. But too
many of us have made such an obsession of self-improvement that we've failed to respond to the crying needs of
the world. There are many ways to integrate the demands
of spiritual growth with the demands of citizenship and
many ways to answer the call to service. If your mission
is not obvious, turn within; get out of the way and listen
for the whispers of your better self. But don't be surprised
if you also hear the voice of resistance. Your ego might
hold on for dear life, placing before you all the needs and

debating the proper response to evil—including whether evil is the proper term to use.

Such challenges occur not only in the face of collective nightmares, but also in our private lives when our survival or the well-being of our loved ones is threatened. At such times we are forced to apply our values and test our beliefs. Hard distinctions have to be made. Where do you draw the line between being pure and being effective? Between patience and action? Between tolerance and taking a stand? Between principled nonviolence and practical self-defense? Between being nonjudgmental and having strong moral principles? You'll have to be the judge.

desires that cry out for attention. You might hear things like "Why bother? What's in it for you anyway? You're too busy. Besides, how much good can little old you possibly do?"

In whatever capacity you serve, no matter how seemingly small the arena, if you approach it with a pure heart it will stand as an important contribution. "Do not overlook tiny good actions, thinking they are of no benefit," said the Buddha. "Even tiny drops of water in the end will fill a huge vessel." As for the question "What's in it for you?" the answer is grace. If you offer your service with no thought of personal gain, the huge vessel of your soul will fill to overflowing.

TRAVEL TIPS

1. *Keep your ego out of it.* "It is not how much we do," Mother Teresa once said, "but how much love we put into the doing." Can you bring to your service a purity of purpose and intent? Can you do it as though it were an act of worship? You might want to check your motives. Ask yourself this: Would I do this service if no one else knew about it?

2. *Protect yourself.* Some people get so carried away by selfless service they become martyrs, jeopardizing their own needs or those of their families. We all have our limits. What are yours?

3. *Don't neglect your practices.* Service can be an important component of a spiritual repertoire, but it should not be considered a replacement for prayer, meditation, contemplation, and other exercises that nourish your soul. Practices are not only sanctuaries from the trials of the world, they are also staging areas where we prepare for action by raising our awareness, opening our hearts, and connecting to the source of all energy and strength.

4. *Enjoy it.* To qualify as service, an activity does not have to be arduous, somber, or sacrificial. Sometimes the best way to serve is to take an activity you enjoy and do well—a profession, a hobby, a passion—and offer it for the benefit of others.

5. Contemplate this verse by Rabindranath Tagore:

> *I slept and dreamt that life was joy,*
> *I woke and saw that life was service,*
> *I acted and behold!*
> *Service was joy.*

YOU'RE
ALREADY
THERE

Come with me to the palace of nowhere,
where all the many things are one.
—Chuang-Tzu

The car is going down the road
but the road is inside the car.
—Bawa Muhaiyadeen

Some say there is no path because there's nowhere to get to. There is no goal, because what we're looking for is already here, and what we want to be we already are. Yet the business of realizing our eternal Is-ness takes time and effort. We need dedication and persistance. But we can't overdo it because excess zeal will slow us down. We need fortitude and faith when the road gets bumpy. But we need to be easy with it all: no worry, no hurry. So it goes on the pathless path to the gateless gate.

THERE'S A
LONG WAY
TO GO

22

NO EXIT,
NO U-TURNS,
NO STOPPING

*To know the sweetness of the Infinite within us.
That is the cause, the reason, the purpose,
the only purpose of our being.*
—Nicholas of Cusa

The spiritual path is not like a freeway you can exit or a job you can quit or a marriage you can end by signing a document. Even if you want to call it quits, you can't. To be human is to be developing spiritually in the same sense that being an H_2O molecule in a river is to be on your way to the ocean. The urge to end the separation from our Source—or, more accurately, the *illusion* of separation—is a power we can no more easily ignore than the urge to breathe. Every pleasure we chase, every thrill we pursue, every joy we lust after is just a badly aimed attempt to transcend our fragmented selves and melt into Oneness. We are driven toward the Divine as a kitten is driven to become a cat, because it is what we are. We are infant divinities, seeds of the sacred mystery we call God, and the longing that drives the spiritual quest is nothing more than the urge to grow up and be what we really are.

Whereas most people are not conscious of the spiritual hunger that underlies their drives and urges, readers of books like this one have a pretty good idea of what they're after. How strong is your commitment to spiritual growth? Are you content with your rate of progress, or are you prepared to invest more time and passion? To advance you have to want advancement. Some say you have to want it badly: "And ye shall seek me, and find me, when ye shall search for me with all your heart" (Jeremiah 29:13). In India, the following story is often told: A seeker goes in search of a master. Upon meeting a highly regarded guru, he bows before him and pleads, "Take me as your disciple, I want to know God." Without a word, the master leads the would-be student to the river and promptly shoves his head under the water—and holds it there as the young man struggles to get free. Finally, he allows him to surface. "What did you want most when you were under the water?" he asks.

"I would have done anything for a breath of air."

"When you feel that way about God," says the master, "then you will find him."

> *What we are looking for is what is looking.*
> —*St. Francis of Assisi*

You will hear many spiritual teachers argue this: You are what you are trying to become, and you were never *not* that, so stop this foolish striving. It is not a matter of becoming but of being; not a matter of discovering something but of recognizing what is. What you seek is eternally present as the Self. Among the many metaphors used to describe this condition is this one from the 20th-century teacher Swami Satchidananda: "Our original nature is like a pendant we wear around our neck during the day and then take off at night before sleeping. One evening we forget to take the pendant off, and then in the morning we begin to search frantically for it, even though we still have it on. Finally, after hours of searching, we go to the bathroom to brush our teeth, see the pendant in the mirror, and exclaim, 'My God, I've been searching for hours, and I've been wearing it all the time.'"

Saying we have to *get* to enlightenment or *attain* liberation or *find* God is like saying that a rose has no scent when your nose is stuffed. It's not a question of finding something out there, but of removing our own obstacles—lifting the veil, to use a common image, to reveal what we could not see before. That is why it is called realization, implying a Eureka! experience; or awakening, implying that we have to wake up from our dream and see reality; or enlightenment, implying that we need to shine a light on what's in front of us. The way of the spirit has been called a pathless path and a gateless gate, suggesting that there is nothing separating "here" from "there." It only seems as though there is—until we're on the other side and realize that we never went anywhere.

People have taken these enigmatic descriptions to mean that it is foolish to think of spirituality as something that requires effort. You're already enlightened. Just snap out of it! There is truth in such ideas, but they can easily become excuses for spiritual sloth.

The same sages who have told us there is nowhere to go have also used images of going someplace, like that of the raft that transports seekers from the shore of ignorance to the shore of knowing. Waking up implies movement, even if the distance traveled is less than the length of a synapse. If there were really nothing to be done, the masters would not have developed the practices that have greased the wheels of seekers for centuries. They would not have made distinctions between various stages of development. They certainly would not have urged us to be industrious about our spiritual growth. The same Buddha who reportedly said upon his own awakening, "How wonderful, how wonderful, all things are enlightened just as they are!" also told his disciples, on his deathbed, "Work out your salvation with diligence."

It is true that some people have slipped into God-consciousness seemingly out of the blue. Call it amazing grace, a gift from a deity, the happy culmination of karma, good genes, or blind luck. It does happen. In many cases, if you look a little closer, you'll find that while the crowning moment seemed to arise as spontaneously as a hiccup, a good deal of spiritual work had been done prior to that. Would it have happened otherwise? Who can say? What *can* be said is that leaving it up to spontaneous combustion is like pinning your hopes of making your mortgage payment on the lottery.

The question of whether there is an end point to spiritual development is debatable, and probably unanswerable. The question of whether it is proper to use terms like "path" and "goal" is also debatable. But as long as we feel incomplete, as long as we yearn for more peace, more love, more joy, more God, we are not *there* yet, wherever "there" might be. On one level, it is pathless, but on *our* level, there is a path to be tread. It may be just a matter of waking up, but we have to overcome the forces that keep us asleep.

The story is told of Gampopa, a disciple of the great Tibetan sage Milarepa. When, after many years, the time came for Gampopa to go his own way, he asked for final instructions. "What is needed is more effort," said Milarepa, "not more teachings." Upon which, he turned his back and lifted his robe, revealing his naked buttocks. This was not a mooning by a master of crazy wisdom. Milarepa was illustrating his point about effort, for his behind was as scarred and calloused as the hands of an old laborer, the result of many years of sitting on rocks in deep meditation.

> *Let the one who seeks not stop seeking until he finds.*
> —*Jesus (The Gospel of Thomas)*

If you want to grow spiritually, attention must be paid. And intention must be made. Only when the yearning for the Ultimate is recognized, acknowledged, and declared to be a high, if not the *highest*, priority can your internal operating systems guide you in the right direction. And you have to maintain readiness, or else you won't persist when doubts, frustrations, and apparent setbacks arise.

At times you'll feel like Sisyphus, rolling the rock of spiritual hope up the steep, rubble-strewn path, only to have the relentless gravity of humdrum existence drag you back down. You might feel that all your effort to reach the pinnacle has been for naught—what the Desert Fathers called the "mid-day devil"—and you'll want to head for the flatlands, where materialism and earthly pleasures

STAY IN THE
MIDDLE LANES

*Going to extremes is never best, for if you make a blade
too sharp, it will become dull too quickly.*
—Lao Tzu

Like the body, the spirit craves equilibrium. Sometimes, if
you've strayed too far to one side of a paradox, the necessary
antidote seems to be to leap to the other extreme. But if
you're dancing on a razor's edge, you need a good sense of
balance. Go to the other side, but not too far or you'll tumble
into the abyss.

The biggest disasters I've seen have involved seekers who
go to excess in everything related to their spiritual pursuit—
especially those who get stuck in the pits of the pendulum,
swinging from one extreme to the other: from piety to ne-

rule. But, while it may not seem so, you're always closer
to the top than you were the day before. It's just that
progress, like growing up, is not always painless and not
always fun. Unless you're prepared to abandon the whole
enterprise, you have no choice but to rededicate yourself
and carry on.

You also need persistence when things are going *well*.
Otherwise, you'll settle for some pleasant intermediary
state instead of forging on to higher levels. I was once on
a hiking trail in the Alps, following handwritten directions
to a viewpoint that the hotel concierge had recommended.
Because my French was strictly out of a phrase book, I
didn't quite understand the instructions. I found myself at

glect; from celibacy to promiscuity; from renunciation to hedonism; from pure devotion to fuming rebellion.

Every tradition counsels moderation. Buddhism is known as the Middle Way because the young zealot who would become the Buddha became disillusioned by asceticism. Had the Bhagavad Gita been available at the time, he might have learned that the yogic path is for those who are "moderate in eating and in recreation, moderate in actions, moderate in sleep and wakefulness." The Jewish mystics said that even moderation has to be practiced in moderation; they called extreme renunciation a form of self-indulgence.

Moderation may seem unexciting, but drama is not necessarily an advantage on the spiritual path. On every highway there is both a minimum speed and a maximum speed. What are your limits? Here are some new mantras to try out: Determination, yes; extremism, no. Persistence, yes; fanaticism, no. Commitment, yes; obsession, no.

a spot with a lovely vista of a meadow bedecked in gold and purple wildflowers. I ate my lunch, soaked up my *vue spectaculaire*, and started back to the hotel. Just then, two hikers passed by on their way down the path, babbling ecstatically, in English, about the magnificent view of snow-capped peaks about half a mile further uphill.

I've used my memory of the *truly* spectacular view to remind me never to rest on my spiritual laurels. You'll reach plateaus that feel magnificent. Soak them up, but don't hold on. Says Meister Eckhart, "Whatever state we find ourselves in, whether in strength or in weakness, in joy or in sorrow, whatever we find ourselves attached to, we must abandon." When discontent arises and we feel incomplete, it's easy to stand up and move on. But when it feels terrific, we need to be prodded.

Ramakrishna is said to have used the following story to remind his followers. A poor woodcutter wanders into the forest to chop down trees and haul the wood back to market. He comes upon a cluster of brushwood. As he hacks away with his axe, grateful for his good luck and pondering the money he will make, he suddenly sees a yogi standing beside him. "Go further," says the monk, and walks away. The woodsman completes his work and is ready to return to town, when he remembers the words of the sage. He travels deeper into the forest. To his amazement, he soon discovers a grove of precious sandalwood trees. As he's about to carry his rich load to market, he once again remembers the yogi. He continues onward. Hours later, having found no better wood, he thinks of turning back. But once again he remembers "Go further." As darkness falls, he begins to regret his decision. He takes shelter in a cave. Inside, he lights a fire and sees that the cave walls sparkle with diamonds.

> *Be patient and persevere, and be firm and constant: and be mindful of God.*
> —*The Koran*

In the meantime, we have the yearning. At times it will hurt. You will ache for grace like the seeker dunked in the river ached for air. You'll be tempted to give up the search just to be rid of it. Go further. You will see that inside the ache is the sweetness felt by a lover who longs for her absent beloved. Sink ever more deeply into the longing, and you will come upon the blessed ardor that wants only to unite with the Divine. If you accept the yearning as a necessary and useful part of the journey, it can be like the sound of the sea to someone searching for the shoreline: both a reminder of what you're looking for and a homing beacon that keeps you pointed in the right direction. It can also serve as a practice of sorts. The French philosopher Simone Weil compared the sacred yearning to the wall between two prison cells, on which the prisoners tap out messages to one another. "The wall is the thing which separates them," she wrote, "but is also their means of communication. It is the same with us and God. Every separation is a link."

TRAVEL TIPS

1. *Evaluate your commitment.* Which sentence best describes you?
Spiritual development is my highest priority.
Spiritual development is important, but responsibilities to my family and career take precedence.
From now on I will devote more time and energy to my spiritual development.
Someday I hope to pay more attention to spiritual development.

2. *Examine what's holding you back.* Do any of these statements explain your lack of diligence?
I'm afraid I'll be disappointed.
Deep down I think I'm undeserving of grace.
I want it to be easy.
I don't know where to turn for guidance and help.
I'm afraid spirituality will conflict with my desires and duties.

3. *Read about the great ones.* When you feel that spiritual attainment has not come quickly enough, reading about spiritual superstars is not only inspiring, it is a great reality check because most of them had epic struggles before their breakthroughs. Each story is unique, but they have in common faith, persistence, and spiritual courage.

4. *Get on with it.* If you're thinking "I'm not ready," ask yourself: What does it mean to be ready? Spirituality is not something you plan to do one day, like moving to a retirement condo. You might look forward to devoting more time to it, but don't make that an excuse for doing nothing in the present.

5. Contemplate this verse from the 16th-century Indian poet Kabir:

> *I said to the wandering creature inside of me,*
> *What is this river you want to cross?*
> *. . . There is no river at all, and no boat, and no boatman.*

23

BUMPS AHEAD,
TAKE IT AS IT COMES

Only the weak are sent out on paths without perils.
—Hermann Hesse

Spiritual upheavals have a way of cropping up when you least expect them, as though someone placed speed bumps on a freeway overnight. The road seems to be smooth and trouble-free, and then, wham! *What is going on here? This isn't supposed to happen!* If it's any consolation—and it should be—most of the heroes of spiritual lore also went through hell. Think of the biblical Joseph, who found himself literally in the pits, but who emerges at the end of the story as a favorite of God. Think of Job, whose heroic response to his tribulations is ultimately rewarded, not just with riches but with intimate communion with the Divine. Their bumpy stretches were passages to grace. John of the Cross famously called such periods dark nights of the soul, in which the soul is purified to make it worthy of receiving the light. His memorable description of this divine alchemy reads, in part:

> *O smooth burning! O luxuriant wounding!*
> *O soft hand, O delicate touch.*

That tastes of eternal life
And pays every debt:
Killing, you change death to life.

Spiritual conflagrations challenge our strength and re-silience. But the flames can clear the way for evolutionary expansion, like forest fires that open space for sunlight to reach seedlings and low-lying plants. It is because of such possibilities that Rumi advises, "When misfortune comes, you must quickly praise." If giving thanks in the midst of suffering is too hard, you can at least try to accept what has been delivered to your doorstep, and treat it as a cat-alyst for growth.

The first of Buddhism's Noble Truths asserts that suf-fering is inevitable. This is not intended to produce de-spair or resignation (particularly since the other three Noble Truths point the way out) but to recognize the re-ality of life as it is normally lived. Perfection exists only in the Eternal. In the world of change and relativity, turbu-lence must always be anticipated. If you have romantic ex-pectations of how smooth the path should be, you'd better have a good pair of shock absorbers.

The first step in dealing with a bone-shattering pot-hole, therefore, is to accept it as part of the journey. The sudden death, the illness, the betrayal, the pain—it's real. Now start dealing with it. If you handle it well, the agony can, like labor pains, create an opening through which new life can emerge.

One day, as he was polishing his sword, the king sliced open his finger. As his physician attended to the wound, the king turned to a palace wise man. "What is the meaning of this misfortune?" he asked. The sage replied with his favorite saying: "Whatever happens, happens for good." The king was enraged. How can an injury to the sovereign be good? As the old seer was taken to the dungeon he repeated, "All that happens, happens for good."

That afternoon the king rode into the woods alone to hunt deer. As fate would have it, it was the one day in the year when nearby forest-dwellers were to capture an outsider to their tribe to sacrifice to their gods. They seized the king, only to let him go. The open wound made him an unworthy offering.

The king realized that the wound *did* happen for the good. He released the wise man and begged his forgiveness. "There is no need for apologies," he said. "All that happens happens for good." Even spending the day in a dungeon without food and water. "You see, I was planning to go into the forest, and I don't have a scratch on my body!"

Stories like that are told to remind us that we don't really know what's going on. We know that reality does not always live up to our expectations. What we don't know is that the pain may be saving us from greater pain; the loss may be sparing us a bigger loss; the misfortune may be averting a *major* misfortune. Sufis tell of Muhammad stopping in the desert and removing his boots to pray. An eagle swoops in and flies off with one of the boots, leaving the prophet to walk barefoot over hot sand. But the eagle's theft turns out to be good fortune: A poisonous snake had crawled into the boot.

No doubt you've seen in your own life how miracles large and small can flow from apparent disasters. A business loss forces a decision that leads to huge gains. The fiancé who dumps you ends up lonely while you're happily married to the person you met while mending your broken heart. The near-fatal accident leads to a shift in perspective and a more meaningful life. Of course, life is not a sitcom; happy endings don't always come before the commercial break. When tragedy strikes, you may not be convinced that there are diamonds hidden in the rubble you're cleaning up. But if you believe that the universe is basically a friendly place, you can at least concede that it's possible.

> *That which oppresses me, is it my soul trying to come out in the open, or the soul of the world knocking at my heart for its entrance?*
> —*Rabindranath Tagore*

Acknowledging the possibility that something good can emerge from horror is, of course, a way to gain a measure of peace. But if your process of dealing with a cataclysm stops there, it is only emotional Novocain. The true task is to turn the situation into a spiritual catalyst. Sometimes, people around you can keep you from going that next step by mouthing syrupy clichés to convince you that the disaster is really a divine gift: "It was meant to be." "The universe is trying to teach you something." "It's God's will." In the aftermath of death, for instance, some people try to soothe mourners with "She's with God now," or "He's in a better place." The tranquilizing voice can also come from your own mind, for you have probably absorbed consoling concepts yourself. Of course, anything that brings relief has healing value. But painkillers have side effects when they are overused or relied upon exclusively.

Palliatives can keep you stuck in the first stage of grief: denial. Pain, anger, fear, and other unpleasant feelings need to be felt or else you can't move past them to genuine acceptance, much less use whatever triggered them to accelerate your spiritual progress. Paradoxical as it may sound, feeling the full force of a painful emotion helps to lessen its long-term impact. By absorbing its energy you move through it more quickly and suffer with it less. Once the feeling is felt, reframing the situation in spiritual terms can be a potent practice. It pulls you out of your ego and connects you to the vast immensity we call God.

Connecting with the Eternal, whether by yielding to the divine will or howling at the Almighty or praying for help, enlarges your awareness. You will be prompted to contemplate the cosmic drama in which your life plays some kind of infinitesimal part. If you're honest and persistent, you will end up, literally or figuratively, on your knees in awe before the unknowable mystery of it all. And in that humble surrender, there is a measure of grace.

This by no means implies that suffering ought to be glorified. Sure, tragedy can be a wakeup call for a spiritual awakening. But it is not a required course. We can advance on a platform of happiness rather than misery. Nor does "take it as it comes" equate with passivity. On the contrary, bumps in the road can be a call to action. "What can I learn from this? How can I use this to benefit me or others?" You can't really know if some higher purpose lurks behind the disaster, but you can certainly *create* something purposeful out of the wreckage. The wizardry that turns a negative into a positive is the spiritual equivalent of what martial artists do: Take the force and momentum of an attack and turn it against the opponent.

Not long ago, I lost a dear friend to leukemia. For more than five years, Steve fought the deadly disease with everything that science and the healing arts had to offer. He marshaled an army of family and friends to pray, meditate, visualize, and otherwise support him spiritually. On numerous occasions, as he rallied and faltered, he would express his gratitude to his circle of helpers. And each time he did, he would be showered with replies that said, basically, "*We* should be thanking *you*!" Steve taught us every step of the way with his unflagging efforts to use his struggle as a spiritual opportunity. He even used the limitations imposed by his illness. Here is a portion of a letter he wrote discussing the side effects of a medication: "An interesting benefit of dryness of the eyes: Although the condition is being treated very well with steroid drops, I occasionally need to close my eyes to rest them. Thus occurs a sort of spontaneous mini-meditation. In the momentary absence of visual stimuli, suddenly I am doing nothing, and for a moment, in the absence of expectations, I am doing it perfectly and I am connected to God."

> *Hard times aren't the hurdles on the road to God,*
> *they are the road.*
> —*Martin Buber*

William Maxwell, a highly respected editor, once said of a young author who refused to make the changes Maxwell recommended "Apparently it's a mistake she needs to make." We can imagine God saying the same thing about us. The universe is always guiding us toward our highest good, but we don't necessarily listen. The divine editor's advice gets drowned by the insistent voice of the ego, which wants to write its own biography in its own way. And after we do what we do, and endure the consequences, the wise editorial voice says, "It's okay. It's a mistake you needed to make." The question is, will we listen next time?

If we're at all conscious, we learn from every experience. But we don't always learn the *right* lessons. Too often, we settle for the easy and obvious ones. This, of course, is an important lesson itself, and the only solution is a willingness to keep looking deeper. For example, a friend of mine lost a bundle of money because of some bad investment advice. What did he learn? "I'll never trust that son of a bitch again." A fine lesson as far as it goes, but not enough. What did he learn about his attachments? His greed? His priorities? His vulnerabilities? His faith?

Another mistake is to fixate on what seems to be a "higher" truth while ignoring practical and psychological lessons. On many occasions I have heard statements such as "I was meant to lose that job because something better is destined to come along," or "He left me because God knew it would have been wrong for us to have a child." The spiritual lesson the person thinks he or she is supposed to learn is to trust in God (or whatever power they believe is running the show). This is well and good, but turning every occurrence into "a sign" can be a way of sidestepping responsibility. Maybe something painful happened because you were careless or self-absorbed or lazy. Maybe you didn't plan well. Maybe you sabotaged yourself because of deep unconscious drives that need to be looked at. Maybe you weren't focused on your spiritual life. Maybe you were *too* focused on it.

It is not always easy to determine exactly what the right lesson is. Sometimes there are many, on many levels.

But you are in charge of your own syllabus. If you want to use the hard times to grow, you have to look for useful lessons, not just esoteric ones—and for lessons that make demands on you, not just the convenient ones. Otherwise, life will keep on driving the point home until you finally get it.

In a sense, being on the path is like walking through a house with the lights flickering on and off: We keep on bumping into furniture until we figure out how to keep the place lit. Every spiritual tradition says that we suffer in direct proportion to our distance from the Source of infinite peace. The bigger the chasm, the deeper life's wounds penetrate, and the longer the scars last. As we move closer to the equanimity of divine union, the disturbances are more like short-lived scratches. In the meantime, we have to respond to misfortune creatively, wisely, and bravely.

TRAVEL TIPS

1. When a catastrophe strikes, do you:
   - Blame other people?
   - Get angry with yourself?
   - Feel sorry for yourself?
   - Get mad at God?
   - Use it as an opportunity for spiritual growth?

2. Think of a crisis from the recent past. If it were to happen again, what would you do differently?

3. If you're dealing with turmoil now, ask yourself what is screaming out to be learned? Look beyond the obvious and list all the possible lessons, including those you'd rather not have to face.

4. *Feel it*. When strong emotions threaten to overwhelm you, you might want to run away from them. Instead, sit down, close your eyes, and feel the physical sensations that correspond to the feelings. If thoughts distract you, gently return your attention to your body. Sit until the intensity diminishes. That is one of the purposes of the exercise. Another is to realize that emotions are just waves in the infinite sea of consciousness that is you. Observe what is going on and gently interject this thought: "I am more than these feelings."

5. *Don't try to explain everything*. Sometimes, disaster strikes for obvious reasons. Other times you feel like the victim of covert action: "Why is this happening to me? What did I do to deserve this?" Don't expect an immediate answer—or any answer. It's not as though you can call some heavenly Fed Ex and trace the history of every karmic delivery. All you can do is respond with skill and integrity.

6. *Be grateful anyway*. Even in the midst of horror, the perceptive eye can find much to be thankful for. A common bedtime exercise is to write down five things from the day for which you

are grateful. The Benedictine monk David Steindl-Rast suggests this variation: Every night, say thanks for something you've never felt grateful for in the past. It will keep you on your toes during the day.

7. *Take comfort where you can.* Turn to sources of inspiration and consolation that have served you in the past—beloved teachers, trusted friends, sacred texts, poetry, art, and music. Discussing the power of music on Ken Burns's PBS series on jazz, Wynton Marsalis recalled how his great-grandmother would say that life has "a board for every behind." When it's your turn, he said, "That paddle is going to be put on your booty, and it's going to hurt as bad as it can hurt. And Louis Armstrong is there to tell you, after you get that paddling, 'It's all right, son.'"

8. *Take refuge in the Divine.* No matter how much darkness may reign on the surface, existence at its depths is light. You can access that luminous essence at any time. It won't undo the loss you've suffered or close the door on future pain, but turning toward the Holy can bring you peace in the moment. In the midst of the Holocaust, a group of Jews who were imprisoned at Auschwitz put God on trial. When the guilty verdict was read, the presiding rabbi said, "The trial is over. It is time for evening prayers."

9. Contemplate this statement from Thomas Merton: "We stumble and fall constantly even when we are most enlightened. But when we are in true spiritual darkness, we do not even know that we have fallen."

24

FILL 'ER UP
WITH FAITH

Help thou my unbelief.
—Mark 9:24

At the *hajj*, the annual Muslim pilgrimage to Mecca, the second obligatory ritual is the *sa'y*, in which the faithful run from one hill to another. Tradition has it that Hagar, the wife of Ibrahim (Abraham to Jews and Christians), ran back and forth between those hills seven times in a desperate search for water. Because of her persistence, the angel Jibril (Gabriel) caused water to flow from the now-sacred well of Zamzam. If not for that well, it is said, there would be no Mecca, and perhaps no Islam, for it saved the lives of Hagar and her son, Ismael, whose descendants became the people known as Arabs. The *sa'y*, a reminder to pilgrims to work relentlessly for salvation, commemorates Hagar's indefatigable faith.

Without faith the spiritual quest eventually grinds to a halt because the ingredient that converts hope into courage is missing. You need courage to plumb the deepest mysteries; courage to look like a self-deluded fool to others; courage to press on when your vision is compromised by falsehood and uncertainty; courage to look at your own demons; courage to have your delusions shoved into your face like custard pies. Courage is most required at times that resemble what rock climbers call a "commitment move." These are the defining moments when reaching the next level means leaving your solid perch and trusting that the person or object to which your rope is hooked will raise you up, not let you fall. At those moments, every seeker needs a shot of faith.

No matter how strong your convictions may seem, you will sometimes succumb to a faith deficiency. It might stem from doubt that God exists; from questioning the doctrines of your religious heritage; from fear that your "soul" is nothing more than a biochemical accident; from misgivings about your chosen path; from the suspicion that "salvation" or "enlightenment" is no more real than the gods of Mt. Olympus; from the fear that everything you believe in is really hogwash. The possible sources are so numerous that someone who has never had a crisis of faith is either in a state of grace or a state of denial.

These crises are no more pleasant than getting your wheels stuck in mud. But you have to dig your way out if you want to get back on the road. And if you manage the situation in the spirit of Chinese calligraphy, in which the same character stands for both "crisis" and "opportunity," you can do more than resume your journey; you can accelerate your pace. It is like using the mud delay to give your car a tune-up.

> *Faith is a knowledge within the heart, beyond the reach of proof.*
> —*Kahlil Gibran*

We tend to equate faith with belief in religious precepts. But deep faith, the kind that confers courage and resolve, is beyond belief. The scholar of religion, Wilfred Cantwell Smith, defines it as "an orientation of the personality, to oneself, to one's neighbor, to the universe; a total response; a way of seeing whatever one sees and of handling whatever one handles; a capacity to live at more than a mundane level; to see, to feel, to act in terms of, a transcendent dimension." Such depth of faith does not come merely from nodding assent to dogma.

If you want your faith never to falter, all you have to do is refuse to question received wisdom or challenge your own assumptions. But if, as Socrates said, the unexamined life is not worth living, then the unexamined belief is not worth believing—especially on the spiritual path, which demands a steel-like faith forged in the crucible of rigorous scrutiny. If we're willing to follow the truth wherever it leads, what we call a crisis of faith can be a sign of spiritual strength, not weakness; of maturity, not regression; of courage, not spinelessness.

Faith gets challenged when something you hold to be true doesn't match your experience, as when a child who's waiting for Santa sees dad put on a red suit and a fake white beard. Something has to give. "Faith is the final triumph over incongruity," said theologian Reinhold Niebuhr, and incongruity is inevitable on the spiritual path, because growth brings experience and knowledge that challenge our certainties. You can dismiss the cognitive dissonance with pat answers. You can rationalize away your doubt. Or you can face it head-on and use it as a steppingstone to higher wisdom.

If you're having a crisis of faith, you couldn't ask for better company. Every major transformation in religious history was led by a spiritual genius who turned a breakdown of faith into a breakaway. Moses, Jesus,

Muhammad, Buddha—every one of them struggled with established doctrine or their personal relationship with the Divine (or both). So did Martin Luther and other reformers who turned the major faiths into a mosaic of sects. It is only by courageously confronting the disparity between belief and experience that a crisis of faith can be resolved, and it is only with fruitful resolution that we can take giant steps on the path.

> *There lives more faith in honest doubt,*
> *Believe me, than in half the creeds.*
> —*Alfred, Lord Tennyson*

Some crises of faith arise not so much from doubts about religious precepts, but directly from the longing of the soul. "Where is the love of God already?" "Where is my bliss?" "What's holding up my supreme awakening?" The disparity between expectation and reality brings up questions such as: "Maybe I'm on the wrong path. Maybe I was sold a bill of goods. Maybe all this spiritual stuff is a bunch of bull." It calls into doubt some of the bedrock articles of faith: that the separation between I and Thou can be ended; that God can be known; that the promises of sages and seers are not just empty slogans or high-ticket items available only to the elite.

Such crises can prompt a fresh evaluation of your practices, your allocation of time, the people with whom you associate, and other elements of your spiritual life. It might be time to make some changes. But it might also be a good time to evaluate the way you evaluate your progress. In this regard, we tend to fall into three common traps: expecting too much too soon, comparing ourselves to others, and using faulty landmarks.

The first two can be dismissed tersely: Don't do it.

We each progress at our own rate, in our own way. Nothing is more futile than to expect instantaneous enlightenment or to covet the (alleged) spiritual status of others. As for faulty landmarks, some have already been discussed: expecting spirituality to instantly dispel our psychological baggage; equating progress with getting what we want; thinking growth means the absence of misfortune. Such false criteria can lead to the impression that you are idling when, in fact, you are coasting along quite nicely.

One category of landmarks deserves special mention: what we might call the Burning Bush School of Spirituality. Many seekers attach inflated importance to spectacular experiences, such as visions, visits from angelic beings, auditory messages from God or disembodied entities, out-of-body transport to astral planes, psychic powers, and so forth. A variation on this is the Amazing Grace or Instant Satori School, in which seekers crave a sudden flash of illumination, a bolt-of-lightning awakening, a born-again, road-to-Damascus, Hallelujah Chorus epiphany that will transport them from lost to found and darkness to light. This is tantamount to turning the spiritual path into a theme park.

Here are some of the dangers of equating exceptional experiences with higher consciousness or nearness to God:

Flashy incidents are just that: incidents. They may be rare, and they may be spectacular, but they are just as flecting as any worldly pleasure.

They can lead to spiritual pride and delusions of grandeur. Beware of thoughts like "This doesn't happen to everyone. I must be special."

They can give rise to attachment. If you're seduced by their charms, you'll want more of them; you'll cling to them and you'll try to get them back when they're gone. How is that different from any other attachment?

They can be distractions. Thrilling, perhaps, and possibly ecstatic. But the rush can be disempowering. Unlike highs you *know* have nothing to do with spirituality, these are often taken to *be* spirituality. If you see them as the be-all and end-all, you'll exit the path at the wrong landmark and forget to get back on.

They can cause imbalance. I've met delightful, happy eccentrics who were fascinated by the occult and others who were so obsessed that their lives fell apart from neglect. One friend became so enticed by psychic powers that his wife left and he couldn't pay his bills. But, by golly, he knew that my long-dead grandfather was trying to tell me something.

You can attribute undeserved spiritual stature to those with remarkable abilities. Says Andrew Harvey of those who make this error: "They take these powers and experiences to be unmistakable signs of divine presence and go on worshipping as divine these people who have, in fact, shown that they are neither good, nor kind, nor humble, nor generous."

They don't necessarily bring peace, love, wisdom, bliss, or any of the other treasures we really yearn for.

Every reputable tradition warns against getting enticed by razzle-dazzle. Some call occult phenomena the work of the devil. Others simply dismiss them as distractions. The story is told of a teacher named Bankei who was challenged by a jealous priest to match his master's miraculous powers. Said Bankei, "My miracle is that when I feel hungry I eat, and when I feel thirsty I drink." The traditional criteria for gauging the "fruits of the spirit" seem to be rather unspectacular: more contentment, joy, compassion, peace, humility, love; less selfishness, narcissism, fear, pettiness, ego. The standards indicate a growing intimacy with the Divine and the best of reasons to keep the faith.

There is also, of course, the option of having *no* criteria. Even the best of measures can feed the ego if you happen to meet them—and produce an unnecessary crisis of faith if you don't. It's important to remember two things: 1) You are where you are, and you can't be anywhere else, and 2) advancing spiritually can feel so natural, so simple, so unglamorous that you can easily underestimate how far you've come.

> *All shall be well, and all shall be well, and all manner of thing shall be well.*
> —*Juliana of Norwich*

Ironically, it takes a certain leap of faith to tackle a crisis of faith head-on. You must have faith that you can resolve the impasse and that the outcome, whatever it is, will move you closer to the Ineffable. Such faith requires, first of all, faith in yourself: You have to believe that you have the wherewithal and the spiritual merit to stake a claim to the light even in the midst of utter darkness. You also have to trust that the universe is, deep down, friendly, safe, and leaning in the direction of goodness. This is the abiding trust of the J. D. Salinger character who said, "For the faithful, the patient, the hermetically pure, all the important things in this world—not life and death perhaps, which are merely words, but the important things—work out rather beautifully." Above all, you need faith in the contention that grace, salvation, realization, or whatever you call spiritual fulfillment is, in spite of it all, possible. That is the anchoring faith that keeps the quest going even when the fabric of belief gets torn. It is a faith that sees doubt coming toward it and, instead of putting up its dukes or running away, takes it by the hand and says, "May I have this dance?"

TRAVEL TIPS

1. *Draw on the past.* Chances are you've survived crises of faith before. Look back on those periods to see what you can learn. How did you get back on track? What did you read? With whom did you speak? Remember as well your sacred moments and graceful passages. The most enduring faith is built on convincing spiritual experience. Recall the times when you felt the palpable presence of the Divine.

2. *Examine your resistance.* What's keeping you from making a leap of faith? Does it seem like too big a risk? Are you afraid you'll lose something? What don't you trust?

3. *Debate your doubts.* Sit quietly, relax, and imagine you're in a courtroom. Imagine an adversary playing devil's advocate—or play that role yourself and imagine someone else arguing on behalf of faith. Give free expression to each side and come to some finality—even if the verdict is that the argument can't be settled. At least not yet.

4. *Turn to the experts.* Examine the lives of saints and enlightened ones. Think of them as scientists whose experiments in consciousness offer proof of hypotheses you can't yet verify yourself. Also, read spiritual memoirs by ordinary people.

5. *Define your standards.* Which landmarks do you use to gauge your spiritual progress?

Answered prayers	Oneness
Compassion	Psychic powers
Detachment	Surrender
Ecstatic experiences	Universal love
Inner peace	Visions
Joy	Worldly success

6. Take some time to contemplate the wisdom of faith in "Peanuts." Charlie Brown asks Lucy if falling leaves make her sad. "Absolutely not," she says. "If they want to fall I say let them fall. In fact, falling leaves are a good sign. It's when you see them jumping back onto the trees that you're in trouble."

25

MAKE REGULAR
PIT STOPS

Exultation is the going
Of an inland soul to sea,
Past the house—past the headlands—
Into deep Eternity.
—Emily Dickinson

Not long ago, I ran into a radiant man in his 80s. He greeted me with a vigorous embrace. "You gave me the ore for my golden years," said Max. We first met a number of years earlier, he explained, when he was about to retire from a distinguished legal career. Stressed-out, recovering from heart surgery, and wondering what life was all about, he let his wife drag him to a lecture on meditation. I happened to be the speaker, and I must have had my glow on because Max thought, "Whatever that guy has, I want it." He made a commitment to spiritual practice that has evidently served him well.

Afterward, I reflected on the lecturer who had so impressed Max. "*I* want what that guy had," I thought.

Back then, my living link to the Divine was strong. I was meditating as much as two hours a day, often adding a lengthy routine of yoga and breathing exercises. I was also taking frequent retreats in pristine locations. In later years, my single-minded focus was diminished by the demands of "real life." What started out as compromises became the new routine. Now I have to make an effort to find time for even that much.

For the most part, I manage to do it. And that, for me, is the key to sustaining progress on the path. Because we have within us what Meister Eckhart called "the seed of God," moving toward the full realization of our divine potential is as natural for us as it is for apple seeds to grow into fruit-bearing trees. But, just as nature's seeds need the proper conditions—soil, sun, water, and what Eckhart called "an intelligent and hard-working farmer"—we have to set aside time to nourish and fertilize our "God-seed."

> You're bound to become a Buddha if you practice.
> If water drips long enough even rocks wear through.
> —Shih-wu

While the great traditions address how we ought to behave in the world, their often-unappreciated essence is to direct us inward. If you were to take from the Bible what I regard as its two most profoundly practical sentences, one from each testament, you would have a pretty good synopsis of perennial wisdom: "Be still and know that I am God" (Psalm 46:10), and "Behold, the kingdom of God is within you" (Luke 17:21). The rest is elaboration, beginning with "Meditate in your heart upon your bed, and be still" (Psalm 4:4) and "When you pray, go into your inner room, close your door and pray to your Father who is in secret . . ."(Matthew 6:6).

There are, of course, a wealth of inward practices. The terms given to the three most common types—contemplation, prayer, and meditation—are often defined in conflicting and overlapping ways. It's useful to keep in mind the following distinctions.

Contemplation generally refers to the act of thinking about something. It implies reflection and analysis. The object of contemplation might be a story, passage, or phrase from scripture; an enigmatic religious term such as "grace" or "God"; a concept such as divine love; a mysterious phenomenon such as death; or a puzzling, perhaps unanswerable question such as the koans of Zen or "If God is love, why do we suffer?" This category might also include practices of self-inquiry such as those associated with Advaita Vedanta, in which the fundamental question is "Who am I?"

Prayer as it is usually practiced is a form of communication with some form of higher intelligence, whether a spirit, a saint, a deity, or the Supreme Being. The familiar kneeling-at-the-bedside type of prayer is most often petitionary in nature: The person is asking for something. There are myriad other forms of prayer as well, such as: bargaining, expressing remorse, appealing for forgiveness, requesting guidance, and exulting in praise, thanksgiving, and adoration.

Meditation is perhaps best distinguished from the others as a nonlinear practice. Think of it as a process of letting go and sinking to the depths of the mind, as opposed to swimming on the surface. It usually involves the use of a mental instrument—a phrase, a mantra, an image—or placing one's attention on the breath or parts of the body. The aim of most meditation practices is to quiet the mind and allow it to settle into its own essence, the infinitely vast, content-free state of pure consciousness. The Upanishads describe it this way: "When all the senses are stilled, when the mind is at rest, when the intellect waivers not—then, say the wise, is reached the highest state."

The distinctions between these three types of practices are important, but the terminology gets muddled and the names are often used interchangeably. What matters most is that each type of practice can be either superficial or deep, and its effects can range from mildly restorative to profoundly transformative. In their highest expression, they all culminate in the same place: eternal silence at the sacred core of being. Call it the Self, call it the kingdom of heaven, call it emptiness, call it God, but no spiritual repertoire is complete without some form of practice whose aim is union with the infinite Source.

If you're shopping for practices, keep these points in mind:

Don't be fooled by the "it's all the same" mentality. Different practices have different effects. They may be similar in intent, and even in methodology, but they are not identical in impact. Look for practices with an honorable history of proven use.

Shop around. You might find what you need within your own religious tradition. For reasons we discussed earlier, however, you might benefit from exploring elsewhere or within the esoteric branches of your faith. The spiritual market can be overwhelming, but the abundance assures that discerning shoppers will find what they need.

Nothing compares to a real, live teacher. While it's convenient and cheap to learn a practice from a book or tape, try to find an expert who has been properly trained and represents a reputable lineage.

The best practices offer both short- and long-term gain. As with financial investments, you should get immediate benefits when you perform a practice and significant transformation over time.

Much depends on the quality of intention. Do you treat the practice as sacred, or as just another obligation? Showing up with an attitude of humility and gratitude is, in itself, a spiritual practice.

Do it regularly. Every teaching extols the importance of steadiness and consistency. The rhythmic alternation of inner and outer, stillness and action, sacred and mundane, works to integrate those dualities and, it is hoped, eventually unite them.

> *Rituals channel your life energy toward the light. Without the discipline of practice, you will tumble constantly backward into darkness.*
>
> —Lao Tzu

Sometimes practice is its own reward; it brings you peace, wholeness, and other immediate gains. Sometimes you look forward to it because you need relief from the weight of the world, or because your heart cries out for a holy kiss. Other times, it's the last thing you want to do; other obligations seem more pressing or other activities promise more pleasure. If it's not the endless responsibilities that scream our names, it's our incessant desires or the endless distractions of our plugged-in world. Even in the middle of spiritual practice, you might want to hit the "off" button because you remember something that just *has* to be done—or because the practice seems tedious, arduous, or dull.

That is precisely why teachers urge us to commit to a minimum daily requirement and stick to it . . . well, religiously. If you need inspiration think of Venus and Serena Williams hitting serves to each other, or Yo-Yo Ma practicing scales, when they could be sleeping in or spending the fruits of their labor at a mall.

Every time someone tells me that he or she does not have even 20 minutes a day for spiritual practice, I quote Mahatma Gandhi: "I have so much to accomplish today that I must meditate for two hours instead of one." Of course, he didn't have to shuttle kids between soccer and music lessons or get to a networking meeting, and God knows he didn't have to shop. He only had a colonial superpower to drive out of his country, a seething conflict between Hindus and Muslims, and a few hundred million people depending on his leadership. But he knew that spiritual practice can be as practical as stretching a hamstring before a race. It is not just an escape, it is a force of integration, a way to infuse spirit into worldly affairs. How could plugging in to the limitless source of energy, creativity, consciousness, and goodness *not* complement the activities of life?

There is always time. If not an hour, then half an hour. If not half an hour, then 15 minutes. All it takes is some spiritual time management.

Of course, there are always other excuses, such as "I'm too stressed out." Which is, of course, a damn good reason to do *more* spiritual practice. Then there's the opposite: "I don't need it, I feel great." Using spiritual practices only when you "need" them is like taking target practice only on the battlefield. It also misses the larger point: Prayer, meditation, and the like are not just palliatives; as vehicles to the Divine, they are the very soul of our purpose on earth. Then there are environmental excuses: It's too noisy. It's too uncomfortable. The vibes suck. These remind me of the joke about three novices in a hermitage, who settle into adjacent cells. After a year of total silence, one monk is heard to utter, "It's freezing in here." A year later, the silence is broken by a second hermit, who groans, "Oh, my back!" And a cry bursts forth from the third cell: "Will you guys shut up! I'm trying to meditate!"

If you can arrange for optimal conditions, so much the better. But you don't need a noise-proof chamber or a special cushion or a sacred site. All such accoutrements are good, but they're not indispensable, and they're certainly not portable. Quiet is better than noisy, but you can hear yourself think anywhere, and *inner* silence is always available because it is our essential nature.

> *When you get to be older and the concerns of the day have all been attended to and you turn to the inner life . . . Well, if you don't know where it is, you'll be sorry.*
> —*Joseph Campbell*

Now for the inevitable caveat: Spiritual practice should be a respite, not a burden.

While it's important to be earnest, if you're *overly* earnest you can suck the joy out of life. Become too rigid about your spiritual commitments and you can close yourself off to new possibilities. Spend too much time turned inward and you can make a mess of worldly affairs—and, ironically, even impair your spiritual practices.

I used to be so conscientious about taking time to sit—no matter what!—that I crossed the line on a number of occasions, turning up late or ill-prepared for appointments, inconveniencing others, and short-cutting various obligations. Sometimes I fleeced both God and Caesar. It was baseball that showed me the error of my ways. I was traveling on the West Coast one October, which meant that the World Series would be played during meditation time. So, I devised what I considered a brilliant plan. I would adjust the sound on the TV too low to decipher the meaning of what was being said, but loud enough to hear when the announcer raised his voice, signaling that something important had occurred. At which point I would open my eyes and turn up the sound. Needless to say, the procedure rendered me both a half-assed meditator and half-assed spectator.

The experience taught me that it's okay to cut yourself some slack. It's better to abbreviate your practice and do it *impeccably* than to rush it or muddle through with your eye on the clock. It's also okay to give your practice a rest once in a while for the sake of important duties, or even to have a good time. Recreation, taken in the spirit of re-creation, can also feed the soul—and, with the proper intention, any activity can become a form of prayer.

The old saying, "Do it right or don't do it at all" applies to the spiritual repertoire. A master once told a group of seekers that the spiritual process was like filling a sieve with water. When they reflected upon the image, the disciples grew depressed. You *can't* fill a sieve with water! Was he saying that they'd never become full? That it's impossible to fill mundane life with the Sacred? When the students voiced their dilemma, the teacher took them to a beach and threw a sieve into the ocean. It floated a moment, then sank. "Now it is filled with water," he said. "That is how to do your practice: Throw yourself completely into the Divine."

TRAVEL TIPS

1. *Establish your minimum daily requirement.*

   • List the practices you do on a regular basis.

   • How frequently and for how long do you do them?

   • Which ones do you wish you had more time for?

   • Which others would you like to add to your routine?

   • If you had an extra half hour a day to devote to your spiritual life, how would you use it?

2. *Keep a time log.* For one or two typical weeks, write down everything you do and the length of time you spend at it. Then examine your log and ask yourself if you're spending too much time on some things and not enough on others. How can you free more time for your soul?

3. *Cover your bases.* Diversify your practices as you would a stock portfolio. By including a broad array, you will leave fewer gaps in your development and assure that your path is well integrated.

4. *"Remember the Sabbath day, and keep it holy."* The idea of renouncing the workaday world and devoting a full day to the spirit might seem like a grim form of penance. It can, instead, be a sweet, sublime holy day. If not 24 hours, how about 12? Six? If not once a week, how about once a month? Once a season?

5. *Shut up.* You have the right to remain silent. Doing so for a full day now and again is not just a good way to rest your voice. It quiets the mind and draws your attention inward. It also has a way of letting your attention rest in the precious Nowness. Alert your friends and family, disconnect the phone, and savor the holy hush. As Father Thomas Keating put it, "Silence is the language of God, and everything else is a bad translation."

6. *Get away from it all.* It is no coincidence that the greatest spiritual revelations have come during periods of silent with-

drawal: Moses on Mount Sinai, Jesus in the wilderness, Buddha under the bodhi tree, Muhammad in the desert, the Vedic rishis in Himalayan caves. Consider using some of your annual vacation time for extended solitude, whether under formal supervision or on your own. Think of it as an advance, not a retreat.

7. *Seek the sacred spaces.* Most of us have to make an effort to find what used to be in everyone's backyard: the inspiration of rivers, mountains, and pure air. Go to the places of awe and wonder, of breathtaking beauty, of cavernous silence and pristine light. Take your excursions in the spirit of a pilgrimage. Speaking of which, is there some holy site you've always wanted to visit? The Vatican? Jerusalem? Machu Picchu? What's holding you back?

8. *Join a team.* The power of spiritual practice seems to multiply geometrically when done with others. If you're one of the many lone rangers who are turned off by communal spirituality, you might want to give your inner critic a day off and reap the rewards of a chain reaction.

9. Contemplate this description of the ultimate payoff of spiritual practice, from the 12th-century Muslim mystic Ibn Arabi: "He who knows himself sees his whole existence to be the Divine existence, but does not realize that any change has taken place in his own nature or qualities. For when you know yourself, your 'I-ness' vanishes and you know that you and God are one and the same."

26

DON'T HURRY,
BE HAPPY

The seeking after God is an endless process,
even for a saint.
—Yacub ibn Sahid

Jason was in a hurry. A long-time Buddhist meditator
and sporadically observant Jew, he felt that his voyage
to nirvana had stalled, and he was determined to speed
things up. He calculated that he would need to take a one-
or two-month retreat, twice a year, to achieve what he
called "maximum spiritual propulsion." To accomplish
that goal, he would have to earn as much money in the re-
maining eight to ten months as he usually did all year. He
set out to do just that, supplementing his private physical
therapy practice with workman's compensation cases. He
ended up working so many hours that he had to skimp on
the daily practices that had always sustained his spirit. He
grew so tense from overwork and sleep deprivation that
he lost his joy and alienated his family. To top it off, one
sleepy afternoon he goofed up with a patient and is now
being sued for malpractice. Instead of gaining spiritual
propulsion, he's headed for spiritual burnout.

Jason is an example of what I call the Barry Goldwater approach to spirituality: extremism in the defense of liberation is no vice; moderation in the pursuit of enlightenment is no virtue.

The promise of supreme wisdom and God-consciousness is intoxicating. We want it ASAP. And, as we saw in Chapter 22, a sensible amount of eager restlessness can be a good thing. It's when the yearning crosses the line into impatience and urgency that we run into trouble. The hell-bent, goal-driven behavior that succeeds in business is not the proper prototype for a holy quest. The spiritual law of diminishing returns seems to be: the harder you try to speed up, the more you slow yourself down.

The very notion of being in a hurry calls up a multitude of paradoxes. We are told we have eternity to awaken to timeless being, and that eternity is now, right here. "There is no here, no there," said the Zen Patriarch Seng Ts'an. "Infinity is right before your eyes." Ah, but before our unenlightened eyes, here is clearly not quite there, and everything appears infinitely finite. All such conundrums resolve in the Oneness that transcends time and space, but the transcendent Reality is not really *beyond* anything, it is *in* everything. More accurately, it *is* everything. But once again the snake bites its tail, because awakening to the timeless Self takes time.

How much time? No one can say. On the spiritual journey there can be no estimated time of arrival, if "arrival" is even an appropriate term. What is the distance between ignorance and illumination? How long does it take to tear down the veils that obscure the light? The normal arithmetic of time and distance does not apply. Nor do calculations of probability. A doctor can predict reasonably well how long it will take for you to heal from an injury. A linguist can estimate how long it will take to learn a new language. A biologist knows how long it takes for a pregnant female to come to term. But no one can predict how long it will take to heal the traumas of a lifetime or to learn the language of the soul or to give birth to a new, enlightened identity. Liberation, the sages tell us, can strike at any moment like a lightning bolt. Or it might unfold gradually and barely perceptibly, like the dawn. Or, it must be said, not at all.

> *Because of impatience we were driven out of Paradise, because of impatience we cannot return.*
> —W. H. Auden

In the early days of the TM movement, someone asked Maharishi Mahesh Yogi how long it takes to reach enlightenment. He said he's noticed signs of higher consciousness among those who'd been meditating for five to eight years. Somehow, this vague remark was turned into a formula. "Five-to-Eight-Year Program" even appeared in TM literature. It was retracted, but not quickly enough to spare impressionable meditators from taking it literally, as if it were a degree program one could complete in a specified time frame by taking a sequence of classes. The rush was on. Anything to get to there closer to the five-year end of the continuum than the eight. It was spiritual avarice of the highest sort.

At one point in the 1970s, I fell victim to this racetrack mind-set, signing on for a six-month retreat on an Alpine mountaintop. It had been presented as a kind of Concorde flight to cosmic consciousness, and I could not bear the thought of missing it and falling behind my fellow travelers. To pay for the course I begged, borrowed, and . . . well, I didn't steal, but I have to confess, I did do telemarketing. The sojourn was at times achingly dull, at others blissful. Sometimes I wanted to take the first train to Paris; at other times I wouldn't have left my cushion if the room were on fire. Ultimately, it was among the most transformative experiences of my life. But it came at a price. I returned home in debt, with no place to live, no job, and no car (I'd sold it to pay for the trip). I was so stressed out from the difficult adjustment that I probably undid many of the gains I'd accumulated on the mountain.

Now, when I see some wild-eyed seeker looking for an express train to nirvana, I get nervous, because I've seen such haste make waste in people's lives: Their marriage goes sour and they end up brokenhearted; their work suffers and they lose a job; friends get turned off by their fanaticism and drop them. Not, on the whole, a way to create good karma. Some get so fretful over their spiritual pace that they grow heavy with anxiety. Needless to say, this is the antithesis of the peace of mind they're aiming for.

> *When one eye is fixed upon your destination, there is only one eye left with which to find the way.*
> —*Buddhist saying*

Yes, there are things we can do to speed our progress. But spiritual practices are not like notches on a belt or points on a scoreboard. They are not quantitative items with a predictable payoff. They are more like the things we do to draw love into our lives: We cultivate certain qualities, we change traits that get in the way, we put ourselves in the right place at the right times. Our job is to create conditions that are conducive to Self-realization. But, as with falling in love—or falling asleep for that matter—if you're too eager to reach a goal or try too hard to achieve it, you're likely to defeat your purpose. "Uncontrolled, the hunger and thirst after God may become an obstacle, cutting off the soul from what it desires," wrote Aldous Huxley. "If a man would travel far along the mystic road, he must learn to desire God intensely but in stillness, passively and yet with all his heart and mind and strength."

Being excessively goal-driven not only slows you down, it can also destroy your peace and rob you of happiness in the here and now. "In my youthful beginnings on this path I was wildly enthusiastic," one spiritual veteran wrote to me. "I rode bright waves of discovery and freedom, sure that any day now I would be enlightened. Now, after almost 30 years, I feel my heart pressed upon and my spacious mind obscured. This concept of how at some time in the glorious future I shall be enlightened and *then* I can live my real life has been an obstacle to living in whatever light I have now."

It can also suffocate your sense of humor, which is as vital an asset for seekers as a good place to sit. The spiritual path should be taken seriously, but not solemnly. It is a razor's edge, but it's also a pie in the face and a slip on a banana peel and a good priest-minister-rabbi joke.

If, as G. K. Chesterton put it, "Angels can fly because they take themselves so lightly," then impatience and excessive fervor are lead weights.

Hasten slowly and ye shall soon arrive.
—Milarepa

Once again we turn to "on the other hand." The danger in taking too literally a maxim such as "The journey *is* the destination"—or, for that matter, "Don't hurry, be happy"—is that it can easily lead to negligence. I've known aspirants whose go-with-the-flow demeanor seemed on the surface to be a relaxed, unpressured, and cheerful approach to spirituality. In actuality, they were spiritual sloths. They paid lip service to metaphysical concepts but they had no discipline, no commitment, no sense of purpose. Make no mistake, there *is* a forward looking aspect to spirituality. If there wasn't we'd have nothing to strive for, nothing to move toward, and as we saw, growing into that liberated state takes fortitude and perseverance. But it can also be fun.

Why not make it a joyful journey? "Joy is the unmistakable evidence of the presence of God," said Meister Eckhart. Take the scenic route, and blast your favorite music while you relish the views. There is nothing unspiritual about taking pleasure in the delights of the world, for "The earth is the Lord's, and the fullness thereof" (Psalm 24:1). Make time for activities that enchant you. Do things that make you giggle, no matter how trivial or silly they might seem. They're not taking time away from spiritual things: They *are* spiritual things. Maybe that is part of the innocence Jesus referred to when he said we have to be like children to enter the kingdom.

I once heard someone ask a guru, "Does it take a long time to get enlightened?" The teacher laughed. "Only if you're in a hurry," he said. It is worth noting, however, that the same teacher urges his followers to be diligent with their practices, attend weekly gatherings, and make pilgrimages to his ashram. And there it is: Hurrying is a detriment, and so is dawdling; impatience is a hindrance, and so is nonchalance. As with any journey, the spiritual path is most happily and productively traversed by those who can fully enjoy where they are at every moment and still move forward purposefully. It requires knowing yourself well enough to set an appropriate pace. Perhaps, like the bush in which Moses found God, we have to burn with desire for the Holy without being consumed by the flame.

Persevere. Lighten up.

Be diligent. Take it easy.

Get serious. Be happy.

TRAVEL TIPS

1. Do you have a spiritual goal? Write down exactly what you are after.

2. Do you often feel a sense of urgency to achieve something spiritually? Look deeply into the origin and nature of that feeling:

- Is it a deep, abiding, stop-at-nothing longing for the Divine?
- Does it stem from dissatisfaction with your life and a wish to be delivered from it?
- Is it mixed with feelings of spiritual inadequacy?
- Do you envy people you think are further along?
- Are you being as gluttonous about spirituality as others are about money or sex?

3. If you're worried that you're not advancing quickly enough, make a realistic assessment of your attitude. Ask yourself:

- Am I looking ahead to a goal at the expense of present satisfaction?
- Am I focused on future rewards to avoid facing difficult issues now?
- Am I hoping that a spiritual breakthrough will solve all my problems or heal all my pain?
- Is my commitment to spirituality in danger of becoming an obsession?
- What am I afraid will happen if I were to lighten up?
- What's my hurry?

4. If you think you might have become spiritually lethargic, ask yourself:

- Are there ways I can give myself a booster shot? Should I modify my practices; go on retreat; talk to a spiritual advisor; attend services more often; change my lifestyle?

- If there *are* ways to enhance my spirituality, why am I not doing them?

5. Contemplate this famous Zen story: A young man approaches a renowned martial artist and asks to become his disciple. "If I work very hard, how many years will it take me to become a master?" he asks.

"Ten years," replies the teacher.

"If I work even harder, how long will it take?"

"Thirty years."

"But I am willing to undergo any hardship to master this art in the shortest time."

"In that case, 70 years."